Investing in What Matters

Investing in What Matters

Linking Employees to Business Outcomes

SCOTT P. MONDORE & SHANE S. DOUTHITT

The Society for Human Resource Management (SHRM®) is the world's largest association devoted to human resource management. Representing more than 250,000 members in over 140 countries, the Society serves the needs of HR professionals and advances the interests of the HR profession. Founded in 1948, SHRM has more than 575 affiliated chapters within the United States and subsidiary offices in China and India. Visit SHRM Online at www.shrm.org.

Interior and Cover Design: Shirley E.M. Raybuck

Library of Congress Cataloging-in-Publication Data

Mondore, Scott P.
  Investing in what matters : linking employees to business outcomes / by Scott P. Mondore and Shane S. Douthitt.
       p. cm.
  Includes bibliographical references and index.
  ISBN 978-1-58644-137-1
  1. Personnel management. 2. Labor productivity. 3. Success in business. I. Douthitt, Shane S. II. Society for Human Resource Management (U.S.) III. Title.
  HF5549.M5664 2009
  658.3'01--dc22
                              2009012523

10 9 8 7 6 5 4 3 2 1   09-0099

Contents

Acknowledgments

Getting a book to print is an endeavor that requires the efforts of many individuals whose names do not appear on the cover. For that reason, we sincerely appreciate and acknowledge those people here, beginning with Christopher Anzalone from the Society for Human Resource Management (SHRM), whose advice throughout this process has been invaluable—and the entire professional team at SHRM, including designer Shirley Raybuck. We also are deeply thankful to the many individuals who have reviewed manuscript drafts, including our wives, Connie Mondore and Meggin Douthitt, as well as Karen Stamatiades, Lea Soupata, Jeanie Douthitt, Erin Dry, Mark Ward, MD, Bronwyn Bell, John Mercer, Carol Williams, and Gail Wise. Finally, we would like to thank the many great Human Resources professionals that we have worked for, and with, over the years that have taught us so much.

Foreword

In my more than 35 years working at United Parcel Service (UPS), I certainly learned a great deal about how a business that has operated profitably for over 100 years in a competitive environment is managed. The bedrock principle of being able to do these things well is to continually measure what you do—and to do it frequently. At UPS, we made it our practice to measure just about everything, because running a tight, efficient transportation/logistics business was necessary to operate profitably in our high cost-structured business. Measuring allowed us to see how we were doing but to also hold people accountable for their performance and integrity. Regularly evaluating the numbers and setting challenging goals kept everyone in the company on an even playing field. The numbers could not play favorites, and there were never any doubts as to where we stood with our operating performance, our people and our customers.

When it came to measuring activities and outcomes, our Human Resources function was no different than front-line operations in its level and sophistication. Looking back over my career as the leader of Human Resources for an organization of more than 400,000 employees worldwide, I feel that one of our biggest challenges was being able to demonstrate, across all of this employee data, the key areas that truly had an impact on business outcomes and the actual value of HR initiatives (the elusive return on investment — ROI). Yes, the ROI is important, but the ability to show specifically which initiatives and areas of focus are causing business outcomes to improve is the future of our profession — and has to be done before ROI can be effectively calculated. *Investing in What Matters* will give you the tools to help you identify the crucial elements that are driving your business.

I am pleased that the Society for Human Resource Management (SHRM), with its mission of serving HR professionals and advancing the HR profession, has published this book. I believe that the process in this book — which Scott and Shane have used to great success in their professional careers — will fulfill SHRM's mission on both of those fronts. On the first front (serving HR professionals), senior HR leaders will be able to use this book to set their overall strategies based on data and analytics. With this approach (that is well-grounded in science and practicality),

HR professionals/generalists will be creating and implementing initiatives that truly drive business outcomes in their day-to-day work. Additionally, Human Resources (as a profession) will be able to use these practices to move forward into a stronger position as a function that drives the business (and can prove it). Human Resources will lose the perception of being a "cost-center." Organizations, both large and small, will benefit from the application of the authors' approach to discovering what drives the business from an employee perspective that may have been previously overlooked or untapped — the "invisible levers."

Human Resources is always striving to better itself, and I am pleased that *Investing in What Matters* will push the profession in a great direction, show its value, and get organizations to demand more of HR leaders in continuing to drive business outcomes.

— **Lea N. Soupata**
Retired Senior Vice President of Human Resources and Board Member, UPS
Active Board Member, Annie E. Casey Foundation

Preface

Over our careers, we have both held positions as HR/strategy/line-of-business leaders in large and small organizations. We have also worked for many years as external consultants to all types of industries. One common barrier that we see almost daily is the "HR skeptic" — the individual who does not see the value that we as HR practitioners provide to the organization. The HR skeptic appears in many forms — the senior leader who does not see the value in Human Resources, or the front-line manager who sees Human Resources as a barrier to getting things done. Some will tell you what they think; some will not. We also know that, at some point in your career, you have experienced (or are currently experiencing) the HR skeptic.

In order to gain credibility with these skeptics, it is important to link what we do to business priorities. We know that there are data that exist across any organization, and the ability to pull that data together, make sense of it, and connect it to business outcomes is the key to that credibility. HR leaders and consultants must show that what they do has a direct impact on business outcomes. Forget the phrase "seat at the table." We need to get into the minds of leaders at all levels and have them constantly thinking that the HR function is a key weapon to help them achieve their goals.

There are many leaders who are not HR skeptics and believe in what Human Resources does because it makes sense and it is the right thing to do. They will not need to be won over. But, imagine showing them how the things that you do are driving what they are focused on — and just how much impact you are having. Then think about creating an HR strategic plan that focuses on your accountabilities to reach business goals that are beyond just meeting HR metrics. Those folks who already believed in you will become full-blown advocates. Yes, and the skeptics will be on-board too.

This book presents a practical process, which will provide HR leaders, at all levels, what is needed to discover the drivers of business outcomes and show impact and return. Our argument is that by following a systematic process of statistically linking employee data to business-outcome data, HR leaders can create a more effective strategy. The investments made by Human Resources will mirror other capital investments that are made based on analytics and data. This will help attain buy-in from all leaders. By using an approach based on sound analytics (what we call the Business Partner RoadMap™), Human Resources will be able to show its impact and value to the organization's leaders.

Investing in What Matters draws upon years of organizational experience to provide a practical approach of discovering drivers of business outcomes to create and execute effective organization-wide HR strategies. The process is based on our work linking employee data to business outcomes, as well as strong research in psychology, organizational behavior, and statistics. This book provides a precise process to gain buy-in from both senior and front-line leaders, while using analytics to bring together multiple pieces of data from various functions within the organization.

Throughout the chapters in the book, we will introduce 10 principles that have guided us in our work with organizations applying this process. Some of the principles are hard-learned lessons, some are a warning to HR leaders, still others are words of wisdom that we think will move HR in a better direction. The principles are not distributed equally throughout the chapters and some are even mentioned more than once — whenever they are relevant. The goal is to provide some thought-provoking takeaways for the reader.

Business leaders are looking for their HR partners to provide them with advice, tools, and actionable initiatives that will help them secure a competitive advantage in the marketplace. It is our mission to make *Investing in What Matters* the resource-of-choice for HR leaders to discover those invisible levers that will lead to competitive advantages.

Setting the Course

Transforming anything is never easy, let alone transforming an entire function within an organization. Having a strong and proven process will make this journey seamless and lasting. In this first section, we have many goals, but they are all centered on placing the groundwork of the process that we continually use, with great success, to transform HR functions from cost centers to strategic partners. Further, we will discuss the challenges that organizations currently face and how Human Resources can step up and become a stronger business partner for them. We will also explore a case study that gives you an inside look at how to apply our Business Partner RoadMap™ process within your organization, so that your impact will be immediate and be focused on key business outcomes.

CHAPTER 1

The Invisible Lever™

"Our people are our greatest asset." Countless CEOs have uttered this phrase, and some have even made it their corporate slogan. If someone tells you that employees are *critical* to an organization's success, you will most likely nod your head in agreement. It's hard to argue against this notion because it just seems logical. Every organization employs people, and, if no one showed up for work on Monday, not much would get done. So, when someone describes studies that have scientifically demonstrated the link between employee attitudes, employee behaviors, and productivity, you will probably nod your head in agreement again. The notion that people are valuable to organizations just seems to be common sense. Likewise, the notion that satisfied employees are more productive also seems to be just pure common sense.

Figure 1.1 Assumed Progression of Attitudes, Behaviors, and Outcomes

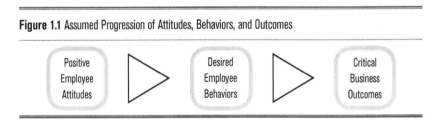

So, why is it that organizations think about investments in people differently than investments in process improvements, machinery, technology, new sales channels, or even marketing? The answer is fairly simple. When a senior executive invests $10 million in developing a new online sales channel, he or she can easily see, touch, feel, and measure the results of that investment. He or she can monitor the new sales from that channel, surf the new web site, and visualize customers navigating the new channel. This direct connection to something real and valuable to the organization makes "pulling the trigger" on a significant investment much easier. On the other hand, investing $10 million in work/life balance programs for existing sales associates appears far less tangible. Such an investment will make them happier and might even retain a few of them likely to leave, but it probably won't significantly impact the Profit & Loss (P&L) statement. But how can you know without proving the value? The bottom line is that the direct impact of investments in people on critical business outcomes is much less tangible — or so it seems.

Principle 1: Organizations already spend significant amounts of money on people ... they just don't spend it on the right things.

The reality is that organizations already spend significant money on employees. Take a look at your organization's annual report. What percentage of expenses are salary and benefits? We would bet that 50 percent or more are personnel costs. This does not even take into account the HR budget, or the training costs hidden within lines of business budgets. The problem isn't that senior executives are unwilling to invest in people, it's that those investments (1) lack data to justify their worth, (2) use the wrong data, or (3) produce unquantifiable returns.

Principle 2: Organizations make investments in people without any data or with the wrong data.

"Causal drivers," for the purposes of this book, are defined as the employee data that are analyzed and statistically shown to have a cause-and-effect relationship with important outcomes. What if we told you that discovering the actual, causal drivers of tangible business outcomes really isn't that difficult? What if we told you that the data for making such discoveries already exist in your organization? In fact, both of these statements are true. Yes, there is the need for statistical knowledge, but, for the most part, the process is fairly straightforward.

Today, the types of analytics required to discover the drivers of tangible business outcomes are frequently used in different settings. For example, market researchers use customer demographics to predict buying behaviors. CFOs do the same thing when they produce financial forecasts or conduct a cost/benefit analysis. These approaches are used because they make an educated, predictive assessment based on facts and data. The goal is to (1) understand the past and to (2) predict the future, basing these assessments on facts and data. Therefore, the idea that *employees' attitudes* can be scientifically and rationally related to tangible business outcomes is not ridiculous. In fact, based on our experience with organizations of all sizes, it is quite feasible — and in this age of intense competition, not discovering the causal drivers hidden in your data silos (we call them *invisible levers*) could be quite dangerous to your business's long-term viability. (When we use "data silos," we are referring specifically to the data that exist in the many functions within organizations *and* that are rarely shared across functions.)

If we accept that the link between employees' attitudes and relevant outcomes can be made and quantified (it has — look at the Sears "Employee, Customer Profit Chain" study in the *Harvard Business Review*[1]), and that we can examine those links to discover specific drivers of the business outcomes, we should consider the following benefits to your organization of making these links:

1. The money being wasted today on the wrong employee initiatives can be redirected to more beneficial employee initiatives, such as those that impact critical business metrics and outcomes (instead of the latest unquantifiable HR fads that promise to make employees happier, more engaged, and satisfied).

2. The investments that you decide to make which focus on employees will result in tangible outcomes that benefit shareholders, customers, and employees.

3. The returns on such investments, via their impact on the top and/or bottom lines, can be tracked, monitored, and quantified.

4. HR departments can be held accountable for impacting the bottom line the same way business or product leaders are held accountable.

5. HR executives will become real players at the table and be included in the conversation since they can now quantify their numerous impacts on business outcomes.

6. Last but not least, employees might just end up being "happy."

There are more benefits, but these six alone are compelling enough to encourage you to apply the approach outlined in the following pages. The purpose of this book is to give you the tools to discover the drivers of business outcomes so that the benefits above may be achieved. From this point on, we will often use the term "invisible lever" to describe these drivers of business outcomes. The term "invisible lever" comes from that fact that most of the drivers are invisible because they have been dormant and undiscovered amidst the myriad data that exist in your organization. We call these "levers" because once you discover the drivers, these levers will need to be "pulled" (applied in the organization) so that they can have a direct impact on the business outcomes.

We will: (1) Define how the connection between employee attitudes/behaviors and desired business outcomes is made; (2) demonstrate the validity of this connection with data from various organizations — small, medium, and large; (3) outline a roadmap to replicate this process in any organization; and (4) provide practical recommendations for senior executives, HR managers, and front-line managers for implementation of this process.

A brief overview of each chapter in the book follows.

The State of Organizations Today

While organizations have evolved substantially in how they view Human Resources and how they acknowledge a workforce's inherent value to the organization, some significant gaps still remain. Measurement in the HR department has improved, but the inability to quantify the people-drivers of business outcomes continues to plague many organizations. This chapter acknowledges this issue and identifies existing shortcomings. Most importantly, this chapter points organizations towards the next phase of this evolution, using the framework and process described in these pages. Organizations consist of different stakeholder groups with different perspectives and needs. When we talk about taking a systemic view, we are describing an overall organizational perspective typically seen through the eyes of senior executives. This perspective is essential because it sees the organization holistically, without a bias from a single perspective. Thus, when decisions are made regarding the organization, they are in the best interest of the entire organization. Further, applying and aligning people-related initiatives at the systemic level creates a culture working in unison on broad organizational issues. The approach described in this book provides a powerful diagnostic tool for organizations — a way to find systemic solutions for systemic issues and become true business partners. Specifically, HR practitioners will be able to use our process to (1) gain senior leadership buy-in, (2) pull together the key employee and business-outcome data from across numerous functions, (3) analyze the data to discover exactly what aspects of the work environment drive business results, (4) create and execute systemic, data-driven initiatives, (5) properly calculate the expected ROI, and (6) re-measure to refine future initiatives.

Putting the Business Partner RoadMap™ to Work: A Case Study

The Business Partner RoadMap™ is outlined step-by-step in an organization focusing on a key business outcome that is costing them millions of dollars in losses. We get into the details of gaining buy-in and putting the data together to show impact. Initiatives and programs that are put into place because of what the analyses reveal are discussed to give you an opportunity to see how analysis is turned into action.

Increasing Sales Revenue

This chapter reviews how HR has traditionally partnered with the sales organizations to support their efforts. We also introduce an initiative for involving employees in the lead generation process to grow sales revenue. Finally, we briefly bring in academic research that has shown the impact of employees working beyond their job descriptions to help their organization.

Increasing Sales Revenue: A Case Study

An application of our process is to use employee attitudes to understand the key drivers of sales in a *Fortune* 500 organization. This chapter explores the causal relationship between aspects of the work environment and sales (in order to increase revenues through employees). The organization we examine in the case study discovers some invisible levers to pull that increase revenue by expanding their scope to incorporate investments in specific employee attitudes identified as critical to increasing sales.

Driving the Balanced Scorecard/Productivity

The link between employee attitudes and productivity is the most popular and commonly assumed linkage. But, as we will explain, simply knowing that there is a connection between attitudes and productivity is useless from the systemic perspective, as well as from the front-line manager's perspective.

Powering Productivity: A Case Study

Uncovering the specific invisible levers that cause employees to work harder and be more customer-focused is explored with another large company. Again, in order to take our methods from concept to practical application to quantifiable results, a real-life example is investigated. We discover the causal drivers of productivity, implement initiatives to drive actions and demonstrate the ROI of the organization's investments.

Decreasing Turnover

A third application that we explore is the cause-effect relationship between employee data and turnover/retention. Organizations commonly assume that satisfied employees won't leave. This assumption always leads to bewildered managers, who cannot believe that their best performers just gave their two-weeks notice. We review typical approaches to discovering the reasons for turnover, from exit interviews to employee surveys, and why they don't work. Also, we briefly summarize academic literature that has created frameworks for understanding turnover.

Finding Root Causes and Solving Turnover: A Case Study

We apply the Business Partner RoadMap™ process in an organization struggling with employee turnover due to the lack of understanding of the critical drivers that compel people to stay with the organization. As usual, organizations that fail to understand the causal drivers of turnover make the wrong investments in people — and the cost of losing quality employees gets higher every day. We will show you how we applied our process to drive significant reductions in employee turnover in another *Fortune* 500 company.

Driving Results: A Case Study for Small-to-Medium-Sized Organizations

The Business Partner RoadMap™ can also easily be applied in small organizations. The approach to using and analyzing data is slightly different, but the overall process and, more importantly, the impact, is just as profound as when applied to larger organizations. This case study takes you through an organization with less than 1,000 employees and is focused on service outcomes that were previously believed to be impossible to quantify.

Breaking Down Data Silos to Drive Results

We have mentioned that the data used with our process already exists in most organizations. Organizations don't make these types of linkages between the sets of data to which we have referred because of the inherent data silos that exist, creating barriers of application. Almost every consumer-oriented business measures customer satisfaction in some form or another. We know that most organizations measure employee satisfaction as well. If that is the case, why don't organizations know exactly how (and what specific) employee attitudes drive customer satisfaction? The simple answer (and complicated problem) is because these data are collected, monitored, and analyzed for differing functions of the organization. We will describe how to systematically break down these data silos to uncover the critical linkages in your organization, which have been lying dormant for years. This book is not designed to contain all of the answers. Instead, it is designed to provide you with a process to find the answers in your organization. The business case we make for following our approach is only relevant if we can provide a step-by-step process for your organization to follow. This chapter will break down our approach into simple, easily executed steps to get you quickly on the road to finding the specific causal drivers of your business outcomes.

Bringing Data Together to Find Solutions

In this chapter, we describe how to use the analytics models from all of the cited case studies to prioritize interventions and investments. The fact is that organizations are complicated and typically don't just have one desired outcome. They usually have numerous key outcomes that they focus on at any given time, plus all of the balanced scorecard metrics on which front-line managers are held accountable. The case studies demonstrate this notion, as one can easily assume these organizations were concurrently focused on increasing sales, reducing loss, and increasing productivity, while decreasing turnover. This chapter will describe how to interpret the information from four distinct outcomes in a simple, pragmatic fashion. Ultimately, the organizations can prioritize initiatives in a way that all four outcomes will be achieved without overwhelming the organization with numerous interventions.

Creating Metrics That Drive Results

The key to following through on your discovery of causal drivers of business outcomes is to create accountability for their execution throughout the organization. This chapter takes you through creating metrics to measure and hold leaders accountable for proper execution of the initiatives that you will build around the key causal drivers.

The Front-Line Manager's View

The perspective of the front-line manager provides another critical stakeholder view. We will spend a substantial amount of time exploring this perspective as it relates to the application of employee data. The limited time that front-line managers have to focus on corporate initiatives makes it critical for HR leaders to use their data to demonstrate the impact that their initiatives have on business outcomes that truly matter to front-line management. While the application of our process focuses on systemic diagnosis and intervention, nothing in organizations happens without the input, acceptance, and adoption of front-line managers. This chapter will show you how to use our process to communicate your initiatives to front-line managers in a way that focuses on what is important to them — driving business outcomes.

Invisible Levers™ for External Business Challenges

Three key external business challenges are discussed: (1) Managing a global work-force; (2) the multi-generational and aging workforce; and (3) the increasing part-time workforce. All three challenges are put into context, and leaders are shown how the process of discovering and implementing invisible levers can help them deal with these challenges and turn them into potential competitive advantages.

Setting HR Strategy

This chapter discusses the transition that will be made in the HR strategy and planning process, when analytics drive HR decisions and planning is aligned with the direction of the overall business. A transition will also take place in which Human Resources will focus more on investments that need to be made to drive the business, rather than focusing solely on how to cut costs out of its functional budget.

HR's "Seat at the Table"

HR executives are often thought of differently than the COO or line-of-business leaders. In part, this distinction is made because of the HR department's inability to link their initiatives to the bottom line. We have created a roadmap for over-coming this shortfall. Being able to show the financial impact of key investments brings with it not only an increased level of importance, but also a large increase in accountability for those results. HR executives should be warned that a true seat at the senior-executive table will bring with it a level of accountability that they may have never experienced in the past.

Trusted Advisor Status

Profiles of HR practitioners that we have encountered are discussed with a focus on the positives and the negatives that they bring to the table. All profiles have important core skills that, if properly harnessed, can help us all reach the coveted "trusted advisor" status. The most important part is that all of these key compe-tencies are needed, but their value must be connected to business outcomes — or else all of that work and talent will not be given the status it deserves within the organization.

Concluding Remarks

Our concluding chapter re-caps what our process can help organizations accomplish and highlights the possible limitations to our approach, if not applied properly. We thought it was important to be our own critics so that our readers would be encouraged to set realistic expectations and apply our process while understanding potential barriers and obstacles.

Appendices

The appendices will provide the additional information that you will need to get started in applying the process in your organization. Specifically, we review: (1) the 10 guiding principles throughout the book, (2) software needs to conduct the analyses, (3) personnel that you may need to hire or contract to execute the entire process, (4) a sample stakeholder interview guide, (5) a sample agenda for a cross-functional data team (CFDT) agenda, and (6) the concept of causality.

CHAPTER 2

The State of
Organizations Today

In recent decades, organizations have evolved significantly in how they think about Human Resources, how they treat Human Resources, and the investments they are willing to make in Human Resources. There are several indicators of this recent evolution.

Take a look at the annual reports of *Fortune* 500 companies, and you are likely to find information regarding the employees of the organization. For example, General Electric's (GE) 2006 annual report states, "With the strength of our capabilities, people, and portfolio, we are a better company today..."[1] The report references people in the same manner as both GE's capabilities and GE's portfolio. GE also uses a strategic framework to organize the annual report, which consists of Financial Discipline, Growth as a Process, Leadership Businesses, and "Our People." The discussion of "Our People" is not as long as the discussions about operations, but, nonetheless, it is there. In their 2007 annual report,[2] GE focuses on employee training and the nearly 10,000 employees that attended their Crotonville training facility. Additionally, there is a lengthy discussion regarding the long-term approach to talent management that GE takes, and the management bench that they keep stocked with highly-trained individuals. This annual report is more than just a series of financial statements, it is also an acknowledgement of the importance of people.

Taking this point a bit further, we looked at the annual reports of the *Fortune* Top 10. All 10 organizations consistently acknowledged the impact of people on the organization's performance. Furthermore, ConocoPhillips went a step further and devoted an entire section of its 2006 annual report to HR (titled, "Human Resources: Providing a Foundation for Success").[3] This section contained comments from Carin Knickel, Vice President of Human Resources, and a brief description of ConocoPhillips' various HR initiatives, such as a talent management strategy and employee benefit changes. ConocoPhillips followed this up in their 2007 annual report with another separate section on Human Resources that focused on talent management, training dollars spent, and participation numbers.[4] In the 2008 annual report, ConocoPhillips discussed "Developing an Effective Work Force," with specific focus on new learning and development opportunities for professional growth.

We also examined the annual reports of the Top 10 *Fortune* Most Admired: People Management. Similar to the *Fortune* overall top 10, we discovered that all 10 companies devoted some part of their annual report to their employees. In fact, Procter & Gamble devoted more than 400 words in its 2006 annual report to employees, placing a strong emphasis on leadership development.[5] The 2007 Procter & Gamble annual report focused on career planning for the top leadership in the organization. In 2008, Procter & Gamble focused on how innovations are led by the empathy of their people. Johnson and Johnson focused on the professional development of its people as a top priority in its 2008 annual report. The CEO further notes that the company's sustained results are a direct result of dedicated employees and management teams. In conclusion, all of *Fortune*'s designated top performing organizations of 2006, 2007, and 2008 thought it important to add a statement or statements in their annual reports that acknowledged the impact of employees on the bottom line.

As balanced scorecards have become the trend in corporate America, so has the importance of Human Resources. Most scorecards include at least four major components: shareholders, customers, internal operations, and employees. As such, in organizations that use the balanced-scorecard approach, employees appear to be as important as shareholders or customers.

Much of the recent increased focus on employees has evolved for several important reasons. First, the evolution of the service and consulting industries has forced organizations to view the people that work for them as one of the primary assets of the organization. It is true that service companies are beginning to recognize, as a fact, that their success will only go as far as the success of the people who work for them. Another important reason for this increased focus on employees has been the "war for talent."[6] As the supply of professional talent has decreased, and the demand for it has increased, organizations have competed over these scarce resources (i.e., people). Companies have invested significantly in the attraction and retention of these human resources.

An additional critical factor has been an organization's focus on leadership. Current wisdom espoused by Jim Collins in his best-seller, *Good to Great*, suggests that companies should grow their senior-level talent as opposed to acquiring it.[7] As such, companies should now begin to invest significant time, money, and resources in developing a bench of talented, home-grown leaders.

Should HR Declare Victory?

We have established that there is mounting evidence that organizations have evolved to think about employees differently. Does this mean HR professionals can declare victory? Not exactly. Let's go back to GE's annual report. In the "Our People" section of the report, the one figure they present is $1 billion spent on training. Including this dollar figure suggests that GE believes it is a good investment, and that investors will also view it as wise. Wouldn't it be nice if the statement read something like, "GE invested $1 billion in training and saw a 25 percent increase in productivity, resulting in a $5 billion return on investment."? Such a statement is possible to make, but organizations still have not advanced enough to make these types of linkages. Consider other questions in regard to GE's annual report: Is a $1 billion investment the precise amount that is making GE successful today? Would $750 million have done the trick? Should it have been $1.1 billion? Without making effective linkages to business outcomes, we suspect a nice round number is what it takes to make Human Resources sound effective. Look carefully at any annual report. If an organization made a $1 billion capital expenditure on equipment, raw materials, buildings, or anything else, you can be sure that forecasts of ROI or actual returns would definitely be included. Why does Human Resources get a free pass? Better yet, is that pass really "free," or does the price come in the form of Human Resources' lack of credibility and standing within an organization?

This example from GE is illustrative of all the *Fortune* Top 10 and *Fortune* Top 10 Most Admired: People Management. As noted previously, all of these organizations acknowledge the importance of their people. Yet, for the most part, the acknowledgement is broad, with a loose linkage to the bottom line. None of the annual reports of this sample indicated a return on investment regarding investments made in employees. In fact, we didn't find one tangible link to a real business outcome. At best, investments were described or processes, such as leadership development, were defined. Furthermore, the majority of organizations made sweeping statements such as, "Our employees are a big reason why AT&T has been named the world's most admired telecommunications company...." — from AT&T's 2008 annual report, with no further descriptions.[8] What does this tell us? Basically, organizations do acknowledge the importance of employees, but they still don't have effective means for understanding the impact of the investments that are being made. It also tells us that investments in employees are *not* thought of in the same way as other capital investments.

Just to be clear, we are pointing out these organizations not to disparage them in any way. We draw attention to the fact that some of this country's most recognizable organizations do intensely focus on people. Our point here is that the process and approach in this book will help all organizations to draw, and quantify, the critical link between people and business outcomes to drive their HR strategy.

We return to the balanced-scorecard argument that employees are just as important as customers or shareholders. The reality is that, in many organizations, the importance of shareholders or customers outweighs the importance of employees. We'll use a practical example to highlight this point. Often, when funding incentive pools or allocating bonuses in a pay-for-performance culture, the shareholder or customer metrics are weighted more heavily, meaning not all scorecard metrics are created equally. Employee-focused metrics are typically "modifiers" of the process, which keeps accountability muddled. Typically, the primary metric is employee engagement, satisfaction, or whatever the latest buzzword is for the employee survey results. But who can blame senior executives for "wimping-out" on the employee metrics? If executives don't understand the linkage between employee attitudes and business outcomes, why would it be as important as shareholder or customer metrics?

We also noted that the evolution of the service industry and "war for talent" have significantly impacted organizations' views of employees. These are, in fact, valid trends in the workplace — but where have these trends led organizations? Consider this: "Accounting for Good People," an article in *The Economist*, discussed how the "Big Four" accounting firms (KPMG, Deloitte Touche Tohmatsu, Ernst & Young, and PricewaterhouseCoopers) were taking a strong interest in people retention. To quote the article:

> Unlike most, however, the Big Four really mean it when they say that people are their biggest assets. Their product is their employees' knowledge and their distribution channels are the relationships between their staff and clients. More than most they must worry about how to attract and retain the brightest workers. Retaining good people is the biggest challenge. Turnover rates at the Big Four have historically been high – roughly 15-20% leave each year, compared with as few as 5% in some other industries. The cost of this is "astronomical," says Jim Wall, Deloitte's managing director of Human Resources. Mr. Wall *reckons* that every percentage-point drop in annual turnover rates equates to a saving of $400m-500m.[9]

Is "reckon" really the best that Human Resources can do? Why not something like, "The intense statistical analysis of the data has shown that a certain drop, or increase, in turnover is directly related to a critical business outcome — and it impacts it by a specific amount"? Better yet, why not discuss the analysis that revealed exactly what is causing the turnover to happen in the first place?

On a similar note, a May 7, 2007, article from *Workforce Management* cited McKinsey & Company as making profits-per-employee their No. 1 workforce metric.[10] Again, this is a great sign of moving toward showing Human Resources' impact on the bottom line. However, this is another metric that does not show what actually causes profits-per-employee to increase or decrease. Consider this: You can slice benefits in half or lay off a substantial number of employees and get an increase in profits-per-employees, but can an HR leader walk into the CEO's office with a list of potential employee investments to increase this metric? Likely not.

In these two examples from the service industry (where the connection of employees to results is the most direct), the linkage of employees to outcomes is still vague at best. Essentially, with balanced scorecards and environmental trends (e.g., war for talent), Human Resources has evolved into a better score-keeper, but still is not an impact player. Remember, the person who runs the scoreboard at Yankee Stadium makes a lot less money than the guys on the field who are actually playing the game and having an impact on the final score.

People Investments as Capital Investments

Ultimately, our process is designed to be adopted by all organizations. People investments should not be looked at as something "nice to do for your people" or "the right thing to do" or even a "great public relations coup." People invest-ments should be as objective as a typical capital expenditure. We don't want CEOs to take emotional leaps of faith in the people-investment decision-making process. Instead, we want them to make the investments purely based on their impact on the economics of the organization and critical business outcomes.

One More Study

A joint study between Deloitte Touche Tohmatsu and the *Economist* Intelligence Unit surveyed more than 500 HR and non-HR executives from around the world and across industries.[11] On the bright side, 85 percent of the respondents recognized that people are vital, and 90 percent believed that people are vital to organizational performance, when they take a three-to-five year forward-looking view. That is great news. Now the bad news: Only 23 percent of the respondents said that Human Resources plays an important role in formulating strategy and impacting operational results. Also, even more distressing, only three percent said that their HR functions and overall people management were world-class. Most of the executives faulted a lack of business acumen as a key obstacle to HR leaders making a strategic impact.

The past president and CEO of the Society for Human Resource Management (SHRM), Susan Meisinger, discussed this study in the November 2007 issue of *HR Magazine* and concluded the following:

"One thing is clear: Business leaders look to HR for much more than transactional expertise. They look to HR to contribute people strategies that help drive business success. Are you making this sort of contribution within your organization?"[12]

Great leaders encourage Human Resources to step up to the plate and make a contribution beyond improving their internal efficiency metrics. Ultimately, HR leaders must show their worth (and not just benchmark data, or best practices) with their own internal data and analyses that show where investments should be made, as well as the anticipated and real impact(s) of those investments.

Who Should Work in HR?

Another important question to ask when discussing the state of organizations today is: Exactly who is employed in the HR function? Human Resources is a true specialization and field of study, and a large number of HR leaders started their careers in Human Resources, with every lateral move or promotion occurring within the HR function. Yes, there are many instances when these specialists were given a short job rotation outside of Human Resources, but organizations paralyze themselves by employing only HR specialists within Human Resources, instead of including well-rounded business leaders as well. The typical lack of focus on the bottom line within Human Resources is a direct consequence of these managers having never been responsible for a true bottom line or P&L function. This is a trap that many organizations have fallen into, and it is not just confined to HR leaders. How many people in your finance department have ventured outside of their offices at corporate headquarters? Having a bottom-line-first approach to decisionmaking will elevate the impact of Human Resources within the organization and maximize the credibility of the HR function. This can be accomplished by having well-rounded business leaders working within Human Resources and by giving HR specialists a lasting and substantial job rotation with P&L responsibilities.

How Much Damage Was Done by "Breaking All the Rules"?

Unfortunately, the one publication that most business leaders and HR leaders recognize on the topic of employee attitudes is *First, Break All the Rules*.[13] The book, published in 1999, summarizes employee survey data and manager interviews across several industries. In fact, the authors claim it is the "largest study of its kind ever undertaken." This statement is probably still true today. Furthermore, we don't really have that many problems with their process. Our real issues with this research, and the book, lie in the basic assumption made prior to conducting the research, as well as the impact the study had on the use of employee surveys. This assumption was that a "silver bullet" exists for employee attitudes — that there are a dozen magical questions that represent the most critical employee attitudes across all organizations. It sure sounds great that only 12 key things matter when measuring employee engagement — but we know better, and we know that we need actionable survey items to have an impact.

Principle 3: Employee engagement in itself is not a business outcome.

Does One Size Really Fit All?

While there is some utility in understanding the most powerful drivers of employee attitudes across numerous organizations in different industries, the idea that "one size fits all" for organizations is overly simplistic. The one thing we know from our training as psychologists, experiences with employee survey data, and experiences as HR professionals in *Fortune* 50 companies, is that people and organizations are unique. Those individual nuances greatly determine each company's links between employee attitudes and desired outcomes. Unfortunately, many organizations bought into the notion that the 12 items in *First, Break All the Rules* captured the most critical issues for employees. As a result, organizations limited the scope of their employee surveys to this short list of items, thereby limiting the diagnostic and strategic value of their employee surveys.

Principle 4: People and organizations are complex. The linkages between attitudes and outcomes have to be understood within *your* organization using *your* data.

Let us use a different example to illustrate the problem with the "one size fits all" assumption. Consider customer-satisfaction data. Suppose a highly reputable customer-satisfaction firm conducts a broad study across numerous organizations and industries, and finds the five most critical drivers (out of, for example, 25 core items across the survey) of customer satisfaction across all of the organizations in the sample. This sounds pretty good, right? Even from our perspective, it provides value to some extent. The problem lies in how organizations have used the knowledge gained from this study to guide their survey process. In the case of employee surveys, some organizations simply asked employees the dozen items in the book and, consequently, action-planned based on those responses. For this customer-satisfaction example, a similar approach would be to ask customers the five key driver questions. Let's say one of those key driver questions is speed of service/ product delivery. This would make sense for retail banking (no one wants to wait in long teller lines), fast food establishments, etc. But does it bear the same importance for health care? If a hospital was following the same logic and only asked the five key drivers (according to the study), it might not ask the extra three or four quality questions for the information the hospital needed. The point is that the key drivers of customer satisfaction vary greatly depending upon the product and industry. So trying to draw macro-level conclusions across industries does not always have that much utility for an individual organization.

When trying to understand the critical drivers of satisfaction for customers or employees, a "one size fits all" approach simply does not work. People and organizations are complex and dynamic. Thus, knowledge on these topics and subsequent interventions have to be contextualized in order to have any real impact. This means that an organization must use its understanding of its culture and people to design a survey instrument that gathers its relevant information. It is good to start with an empirically derived short-list of items, but organizations cannot stop there. From survey design to analysis to action-planning, the process must be customized and contextualized for each unique organization. Obviously, this is just one example of HR data that has to be examined and contextualized when you look at your organization. It is clear that your suite of training, culture, pay structure, etc., are important elements to examine, as well.

Given this need to create custom solutions for organizational research, the approach described in this book will provide a roadmap for this type of solution. This roadmap will allow organizations to identify key drivers of meaningful business outcomes within the context of each organization's unique culture, environmental conditions (e.g., local job market), customer base, and employee nuances. Only with this level of customization can an organization truly quantify the impact of employee attitudes on business outcomes and, subsequently, calculate a true ROI.

The Process for Moving Beyond

As we mentioned, connecting employee attitudes to tangible outcomes is not really that difficult. Before we move on to real-world examples of how to make this connection, we want to give you a high-level overview of the process. (We will provide greater detail and clarity in a later chapter.) We simply want to outline the process so you have a general understanding before getting into the details and case studies. Again, this process incorporates a degree of analytics, but, for the most part, it is comprised of basic organizational development/change methodologies with which most business leaders are familiar.

This process consists of six key steps. (See Figure 2.1 at the end of the chapter.)

1. Determine Critical Outcomes

The first step is obvious. An organization must first determine the top two to three most critical outcomes or priorities that it anticipates will be accomplished through its employees. For example, outcomes such as increasing productivity, decreasing turnover, or increasing customer satisfaction are commonly desired outcomes. These outcomes can be gleaned by reviewing strategic documents and plans. Key stakeholder interviews of the board, CEO, CFO, or other business leaders are also helpful in the process. (A basic interview guide is provided in the Appendices.) Once this information has been collected and summarized, the outcomes must be prioritized into two to three desired outcomes. It is possible for these outcomes to change annually, but it is also desirable to maintain some consistency to track progress and keep the organization focused. The same outcomes will be critical to the organization year to year.

2. Create a Cross-Functional Data Team

Once the various owners of the critical business metrics have been identified, a cross-functional data team needs to be organized. This team should consist of measurement experts, key line-of-business leaders or metric owners, and HR leadership. The measurement experts are needed in order to determine data requirements to scientifically link the necessary data sets and conduct the requisite statistical analyses. It may also be necessary to adjust the existing measurement approach for the critical outcome measures. Measurement characteristics such as the frequency or level of measurement may need to be altered in order to make the appropriate linkage across data sets. This cross-functional team will also facilitate and sponsor the linkage initiative. Therefore, it is important to have influential company leaders and decision-makers participate in this process. (We will further discuss potential barriers to integrating data sets in Chapter 12). At this point in our journey, it is only necessary to understand the importance of this cross-functional team and acknowledge that the necessary data already exist in most organizations.

3. Assess Measures of Critical Outcomes

Once the critical outcomes have been identified, the next step is to determine how data are currently captured in the organization. For example, most organizations measure customer satisfaction in some manner. Several measurement characteristics of each outcome measure must be assessed. These include:

■   Frequency of measurement (e.g., monthly, quarterly, annually)

■   Level of measurement (e.g., by line of business, by work unit, at the organization level)

■   Organizational owners of each outcome measure (e.g., the department or leader of customer-satisfaction measurement)

It is critical to understand each of these measurement characteristics before any linkages to employee attitudes can be made.

4.   Objective Analysis of Key Data

This is the part of the process that actually requires advanced statistical knowledge. Most large organizations employ statisticians or social scientists. If this type of internal resource does not exist in your organization, then hiring a consultant or full-time statistician for this role is necessary. This critical step is where the data sets are linked through various methodologies. Structural-equations modeling is the preferred solution for these types of data linkage analyses because cause-effect relationships can be inferred. Structural-equations modeling allows one to state that employee attitudes about work/life balance are a causal driver of increased customer satisfaction, for example. This implied causality is important for understanding how these different measures relate to each other and for calculating ROI.

The statistical component is not overly complicated and it is a tool for accomplishing three things:

1.   Understanding the relationship between employee attitudes/behaviors and meaningful outcomes.

2.   Prioritizing types of interventions (i.e., determine which invisible levers to pull).

3.   Estimating ROI to determine levels of investments and expected returns.

All of this work is designed to allow you to figure out which levers to pull and how much to invest in them. The final result generated from the data-analysis step is a list of two to three key priorities, taken from the employee data, which will simultaneously drive the desired outcomes. For example, increasing employee attitudes about work/life balance will increase productivity and customer satisfaction, and decrease turnover. We will provide a case study that shows how to integrate priorities across the two to three desired outcomes. Again, this sounds somewhat complicated, but it really is not. Our goal throughout the book is to demystify and simplify the statistical components of this process.

5.   Build the Program and Execute

Once the critical invisible levers have been identified, the next step is to determine what types of interventions will have the desired effect. This is the action-planning stage where activities can be focused at the systemic (organization-wide) level, line-of-business level, or work-unit level. Frankly, this stage encompasses the bulk of work and investment associated with any people-related process. This still holds true in the model we have proposed. The main difference is that the investments being made are focused on those employee processes/attitudes/demographics, etc., that have a direct impact on the organization's desired outcomes. In our model, an expected return can be used to guide the amount of investment made on a particular intervention. Basically, organizations are going beyond taking action to make happier employees by investing in people to provide greater shareholder value.

Principle 2: Organizations make investments in people without data or with the wrong data.

Throughout the book, we will provide some additional tips and guidance regarding this stage of the process. Most organizations that have made focusing on people a priority for several years have developed a robust action-planning process. The key for implementing our process is to leverage the existing process and, at the same time, enhance it. For example, many organizations provide a solid process and tools for work-unit interventions, but are less effective at the systemic level. Oftentimes results are pushed to individual managers, and they then own the action-planning process for their department. Solid action-planning in our process typically requires both work-unit level and systemic-level action-planning.

Another trap at this stage is to look for the "silver bullet" of interventions. Best practices (another name for "silver bullets") are great to guide action-planning. But, simply replicating a "best practice" will get an organization nowhere. Remember our statements from earlier in the book regarding a "one size fits all" approach? This concept holds true for both the diagnostic phases and the intervention stages. Interventions must be customized and placed in the context of each unique organization. Once the intervention program is built, it is then all about execution. Of course, creating a sense of urgency around execution of the program depends upon having clear expectations regarding ROI and tangible goals tied to incentives, for leaders.

6.   Measure and Adjust/Re-Prioritize

The last step is to re-measure in order to assess progress and calculate ROI. Most business leaders understand the importance of goal-setting and measurement. They also understand the importance of creating a culture of measurement and account-ability. For example, measuring employee attitudes through an employee survey every 18-24 months just does not make any sense. A culture of accountability is the reason customer satisfaction is measured continuously in organizations. If we told a CEO that financials would be reported only annually, he or she would laugh. While we don't recommend monthly monitoring of employee attitudes, measuring them a couple of times a year does seem reasonable and necessary. Other employee mea-sures, such as training participation, are measured more frequently in organizations. Learning management systems (LMS) typically provide employee-training data at a higher frequency of measurement (often in real-time). In the cases where continu-ous measurement is available, an organization's ability to monitor progress and drive accountability is greatly enhanced.

Similar to how other organizational decisions are made, slight adjustments (based on measurement results) to interventions should be made along the way. However, it is not advisable to completely change the strategic focus of the inter-ventions. In other words, pick your two to three priorities and build action plans around those priorities. Measure progress against those plans two to three more times, and then re-calculate the data-set linkages and re-prioritize. This should be an annual analysis process.

Figure 2.1 The Business Partner RoadMap™

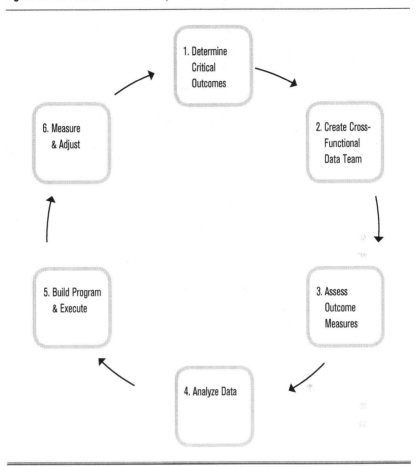

CHAPTER 3

Putting the Business Partner RoadMap™ to Work: A Case Study

Now we are going to use a real-life overview to show you how our approach comes together. We recently completed the first stages (specifically steps one through five of the RoadMap) of a cost-reduction project with a large retail organization. This is particularly relevant because this organization, like nearly all organizations, was focused strongly on reducing costs amidst the economic downturn. This retail organization has been around for many years and was facing the prospect of substantially slowing their growth plans and possibly laying off numerous employees. The need to reduce costs across the entire network of stores was critical to maintaining their plans and employment levels. Cost-cutting is never an easy process, but bringing in HR as a weapon to find areas in which to invest, and where to cut, instead of merely conducting the layoff meetings was key to the success of the initiative — and the organization.

Stage 1: Determine Critical Outcomes

Leaders at the organization communicated about areas of pain that they were experiencing — those areas of their business that worried them the most and held a prominent place in nearly every meeting. The leaders revealed to us that an area that they were attacking head-on with a special project task force was "product shrink." Product shrink encompasses internal (employee) and external (non-employee) theft of merchandise and loss of product due to damage or to becoming unsellable. Product shrink costs this organization hundreds of millions of dollars each year and directly impacts their bottom-line profits. Worldwide estimates put the costs of shrink to retailers at over $100 billion annually — and that is just for theft. That number does not include the damaged or unsellable numbers. Based on our stakeholder interviews, the key priority was reducing shrink. Our focus was on identifying the causal drivers of product shrink.

Stage 2: Assemble the Cross-Functional Data Team

The project task force originally consisted of leaders from supply-chain management, process improvement, customer service/satisfaction, loss prevention, and Human Resources. HR's role was to focus on staffing and involuntary turnover issues related to internal theft — identified as a key part of the company's "product shrink" issue. Of course, staffing is a critical factor, as are terminations for theft control; however, this organization, like many organizations that are focusing on cost-cutting, was not using their myriad of people data to its fullest advantage.

We were invited to discuss with the product-shrink task force, in broad terms, how discovering the causal drivers of product shrink would provide their leadership with additional weapons to fight this costly problem. It was clear that the primary objective of this project would be to understand the people drivers of product shrink.

Since we had already conducted stakeholder interviews, we moved to the second step, which was to pull together a cross-functional data team with our key goals being to:

1. Understand how the outcome variable (i.e., product shrink) was being measured.
2. Generate a list of potential measures that could impact shrink.
3. Determine how each of those measures (independent variables) were being measured.

Our first recommendation was to pull in additional key individuals from Human Resources along with some of their associates from the HR information systems (HRIS) group who had in-depth knowledge of, and direct access to, the people data that was being measured. Our primary focus is typically directed toward people issues and people-data analytics — so it makes sense to have additional HR leaders on the cross-functional data team. We should note that it is not always the case that business-outcome-focused project teams launch with an HR representative as a key member. In too many cases, Human Resources is an afterthought or is ignored. As you will see in this example, and throughout the entire book, these organizations are missing a great opportunity by failing to examine how employee data can be analyzed to show its impact on key business outcomes.

Once the initial steps of the meeting are completed (see Appendices for a sample agenda of an initial cross-functional data team meeting), the best starting point for the cross-functional data team is determining how the business outcome (on which the project team is focusing) is measured. Determining how a business outcome is measured is usually not a difficult step because if the business outcome has warranted its own special project team, then it is, or certainly should be, getting measured with great regularity. We discovered that the product shrink variable was being measured at the individual store level on a monthly basis. The level at which the data are measured is important because, when you are conducting the analysis to determine cause-effect relationships, it is much easier and more accurate if the personnel and operations data are measured at the same level. As for the frequency at which the data are measured, this is important because you will need to keep in mind that the data that you are analyzing as causal drivers must have been measured *earlier*, in chronology, than the business outcome that it is, theoretically, impacting.

Principle 5: The people data and outcome data do exist – you just have to go get it.

Our second goal for the team was to facilitate a discussion with the team members around the key areas that might be driving product shrink. Various aspects of shrink and the essential management behaviors, competencies, and attitudes that would lend themselves to a reduction in product shrink were explored. The discussion then moved to what data are measured with regularity and consistency that would be available to analyze. The HRIS representatives noted that the organization had gathered an extensive bank of people data. We focused on their:

1. Annual employee survey.
2. Performance-management competency assessments for front-line managers.
3. Voluntary training focused on sales and product shrink.
4. "Mandatory" ethics training. (We air-quoted mandatory because, as you know, sometimes "mandatory" training isn't so "mandatory".)
5. Store-level employee turnover.
6. Average front-line manager tenure with the organization.
7. Average tenure in the front-line manager position.

One of the great things about using the Business Partner RoadMap™ process is that you are not limited to examining only employee data. So, in addition to the seven key pieces of employee data examined above, we also examined store-level customer-satisfaction data. Remember, our goal is to take all of this data and discover what has a direct impact on the key business outcome — product shrink. The more (relevant) data that can be placed into the analysis, the better, because we also want to discover if any current conventional wisdom can be shown to be incorrect. This is why the initial stakeholder interviews are so important, because they will reveal what the organization's leaders believe to be causing the problem, and you will be able to show what is *actually* causing the problem (i.e., instant credibility for you).

The conclusion of the cross-functional data team meeting should consist of the team leader (you) assigning the team members the tasks of data collection and compilation. The customer-satisfaction representative on the cross-functional data team was charged with supplying us with store-level data from the previous year. The representatives from HRIS were asked to provide us with (1) the store-level raw data from the most recent employee opinion survey; (2) the front-line manager performance-management competency assessments; (3) the training attendance data from both the ethics course and the sales/shrink course; and (4) the most up-to-date, store-level employee turnover data from the previous 12 months. Once the initial meeting of the cross-functional data team was complete, we relied on the HR leader from the task force to manage the data collection projects and hold people accountable for pulling their data together.

Stage 3: Assess Outcome Measures

Assessing outcome measures means verifying that the data is measured at a level that will be useful in the analyses. For example, if you work in a retail organization with 100 stores, and you have employee data at the store level, then you will want to make sure that your outcome data (e.g., turnover, profit productivity) is also measured at the store level. Having enough data points is a typical barrier that can be overcome, but it needs to be known up front so that is can be planned for. In this project, this organization did a great job collecting data at their store level, as that is how they held front-line managers accountable for performance. This meant we were in great shape to begin analyzing.

Stage 4: Analyze the Data

As we have mentioned, the actual data analysis is where some of the advanced statistical analytics come into play. Unfortunately, we reviewing all the "ins-and-outs" of structural-equations modeling would take away from the value in using what the analysis will reveal. (See the Appendices, for what type of software to consider and where to potentially find people who do know the "ins-and-outs" of structural-equations modeling.)

To provide you some important details, Figures 3.1 and 3.2 show (1) the dimensions measured on the organization's employee-opinion survey and (2) the competencies measured on the organization's performance-management competency assessment for front-line managers, respectively.

Figure 3.1 Dimensions Represented in the Employee-Opinion Survey

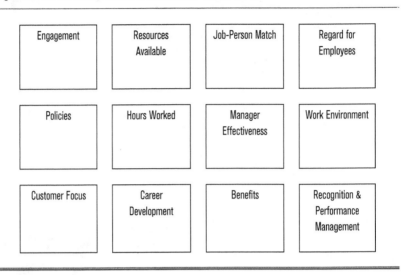

Figure 3.2 Competencies in the Performance Management Assessment

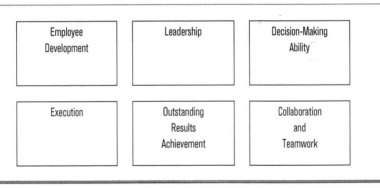

The results of the data-analysis stage are revealed in the Cause-and-Effect Chart in Figure 3.3. Let's walk through Figure 3.3 and point out some critical points.

Figure 3.3 Casual Impact Chart of Product Shrink

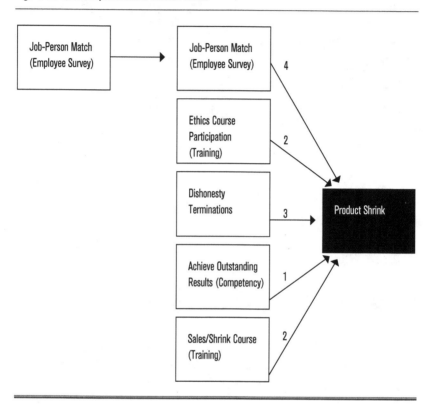

First, the outcome of "product shrink" is on the right side of the Cause-and-Effect Chart and the arrows pointing directly at product shrink are attached to its six key causal drivers. They are:

1. Ethics Course Participation — This driver of product shrink came from the organization's learning management system (LMS) database. The data showed what percentage of current employees had completed the course. If you remember, we noted that this course was "mandatory."

2. Sales/Shrink Course Participation — This driver of product shrink also came from the organization's LMS database. The data showed what percentage of current employees had completed the course. (Note: This is a voluntary course — more on that later.)

3. Dishonesty Terminations — This driver of product shrink was culled from the organization's database of employee turnover. This data represent the number of individuals at each store that were terminated for dishonesty (e.g., product theft).

4. Achieve Extraordinary Results — This driver of product shrink comes directly from the organization's competency model for front-line managers.

5. Customer Focus — This driver of product shrink comes from the organization's annual employee-opinion survey. It is an important construct that was revealed after we conducted a factor analysis of their survey vendor's database.

6. Job-Person Match — This driver is a sub-factor of product shrink that comes from the organization's annual employee-opinion survey. Though Job-Person Match is not a direct causal driver of shrink, it is a causal driver of Customer Focus. It is also an important construct that was revealed after we conducted a factor analysis of their survey vendor's database.

The numbers on the arrows pointing to product shrink represent the level of impact of each of the causal drivers. So, the "1" on the arrow from Achieving Outstanding Results to Product Shrink means that it is the most impactful causal driver of product shrink. This ranking is based purely on the results of the data analysis (i.e., Achieving Outstanding Results had the largest statistical impact). The reason that we rank each of the outcomes is so that we can help the product-shrink task force to fully prioritize the actions that need to be taken.

Stage 5: Build Program and Execute

The goals of stage five include: (1) meeting again with the members of the product-shrink task force to review the analysis that we conducted and (2) determining very clearly the next steps in taking action on the results. As trusted advisors, the story that you tell with the data is of utmost importance, because it will spur the task force to action. Doing the proverbial "data-dump" will not establish your credibility nor will it help the task force. As an HR professional, being able to take the data analytics and turn it into a bold plan of action is a skill that will serve you well. The "data story" should include the following elements:

■ A brief review of the initial cross-functional data team meeting

■ A review of the data elements included in the analysis

■ An overview of the type of analyses conducted

■ Visual display of what data impacted the business outcome

■ Visual display of what data did *not* impact the business outcome (it is important to dispel myths and conventional "wisdom")

- Recommendations on necessary action steps (remember, this is where your expertise in Human Resources comes into play)

We cannot emphasize this last "bullet" strongly enough. When you return to meet with the task force armed with hard data based on a truly stringent analysis that demonstrates cause-and-effect relationships with business outcomes, you will enjoy a very high level of credibility. That credibility now entitles you to live up to a new level of expectations. Bringing a strong action plan to work on the key causal drivers of the business outcome will be the way to meet those expectations.

Now it was time to focus on what the data were saying, and build and execute programs around the causal drivers. Again, Figure 3.3 shows what impacted product shrink. We will now provide you with context and detail around each of the causal drivers and, most importantly, the programs that we recommended that the organization implement.

Impacting a Key Competency: Achieving Outstanding Results

In the analysis, a manager's level of competence in the area of "Achieving Outstanding Results" was the single strongest causal driver of product shrink in the entire model. The "Achieving Outstanding Results" competency from the front-line manager performance-management-assessment feedback process was defined as:

- "Meets or exceeds stretch goals; makes continuous improvement gains."
- "Holds him/herself and direct reports accountable for achieving stretch goal results in sales, store profitability, cost controls, and 'product shrink.'"
- "Constantly pushes him/herself and coaches others toward the highest levels of achieving stretch goals."
- "Constantly focuses on new solutions and ideas that add value to driving sales, cost reductions, and improving the overall bottom line."
- "Uses knowledge of operational policies and standard operating procedures/ practices to achieve outstanding results."

The data told us that (1) higher ratings of front-line managers on the competency of "Achieving Outstanding Results" were causing the amount of losses due to product shrink to decline and (2) this competency was having the largest impact on product shrink. Armed with this information, we then had the opportunity to make important recommendations on what actions the product-shrink task force could undertake while partnering with Human Resources. It is extremely important to realize that our goal is not to put the entire focus on getting scores on this competency to increase — this will inspire the wrong types of behavior and will ultimately cause a "numbers game" to ensue. We want to focus on increasing and improving the behaviors, skills, and management routines that are associated with this competency. This next section will describe the recommendations made to the task force, beginning with "Achieving Outstanding Results" competency — the strongest driver of product shrink.

Recommendation #1

■ On-site "Best Practice" Assessments of the Top 10 Managers in Product-Shrink Performance with High Competency Ratings on "Achieving Outstanding Results"

The focus of this recommendation is to help leaders get a specific idea of the skills, behaviors, and management routines that are being used by the front-line managers who are performing the best on product shrink and on this competency. To get a strong assessment of these key front-line managers' skills, behaviors, and management routines, we recommended focus groups with store employees and detailed interviews with front-line managers. The goals of the focus groups and interviews were to discover (1) typical behaviors/routines and best practices, (2) how and why the best front-line managers were achieving these outstanding results, and (3) how and why employees were buying-in to achieving these results.

■ On-site "Help-Needed" Assessments of the Bottom 10 Managers in Product-Shrink Performance with Low Competency Ratings on "Achieving Outstanding Results"

In the same vein as the first recommendation, it is equally important to help leaders get a clear picture of what managers, who struggle with product shrink and "Achieving Outstanding Results," are doing on a daily basis. The approach and process is the same in that we again called for local focus groups with employees and one-on-one interviews with front-line managers to dig deeper into their daily behaviors and management routines. These actions will lead to a detailed understanding of what managers either should not do or, at the least, should adjust in order to achieve outstanding results in terms of product shrink.

Recommendation #2

■ Product-Shrink Partnering Program
   » Pair top shrink managers with help-needed shrink managers for coaching/ mentoring.

» Hold regular meetings with top shrink and help-needed shrink managers to share best practices.

» Build a management routine to continually focus on shrink and share best practices.

This recommendation is truly focused on creating routines and accountability that will help front-line managers reduce product shrink and maximize the sharing of best practices.

Impacting Training

As the analysis revealed, both the ethics course and the sales/shrink course had a strong, cause-and-effect impact on product shrink. In regard to ethics course participation, we mentioned earlier that this course was mandatory; however, the data clearly showed that not everyone was attending the course. This represented a clear opportunity, especially since the ethics course became an important causal driver of product shrink. If you remember, product shrink includes employee theft, so it makes perfect sense that not participating in this class was causing more losses due to product shrink.

Recommendation #3
■ Ethics Course & Sales/Product Shrink Course Re-vamp and Drive Participation

The ethics course had not been looked at from a content perspective or from an instructional-design perspective in many years. The course itself had very good content but, admittedly, had become somewhat bland and was merely a "check-the-box" course in the eyes of employees and managers. Our analysis had shown that the ethics course was having a strong, causal impact on product shrink — and therefore represented a missed opportunity for the organization. First, we recommended to the task force that they freshen up the content of the course and its delivery method. Second, since numerous employees had not taken the course, and it could have been a long time since tenured managers had participated, we recommended that the organization retrain all managers and employees. Finally, senior leadership involvement and advocacy is always a critical element to a successful initiative. To that end, we recommended that the organization's senior leaders internally communicate the revamped and relaunched ethics course, while incorporating the themes taught in the course into their typical organizational communications.

The sales/product shrink course was voluntary for employees and also turned out to be a significant causal driver of product shrink. The data told us that having more employees take the course at a store was causing the amount of product shrink at that store to decrease.

The sales/product shrink course was obviously an effective course, but was not being used by all front-line managers and employees. Considering its strong impact on product shrink, this was a straightforward opportunity for the task force to have an immediate impact. Basically, we recommended that the task force retrain all managers and employees who had not taken the course in the past 12 months. In addition, we recommended that the course be "mandatory" for all new hires. (Except, in this case, we want mandatory to actually mean *mandatory*.) The task force agreed with us. Both of these training recommendations were implemented with a relatively small investment.

Impacting Hiring

Dishonesty-terminations data were pulled from HRIS and were significant causal drivers of product shrink. The data told us that having more employees terminated due to dishonesty at a store was causing the losses due to product shrink to increase.

Recommendation #4
- Hiring Process Overhaul

First instincts might tell you that having a problem with dishonesty terminations would warrant more surveillance of the stores. That would help to terminate more people, but it is a downstream solution. We challenged the task force to take an upstream approach to the issue as well.

Our first recommended action was for the organization to rethink its hiring practices. We discussed with them the extent that background checks were incorporated into the selection process. Unfortunately, background checks were not the norm at the organization for new hires under the age of 18. Also, new employees were typically hired before background-check results were received. Ironically, the theft at this organization occurred almost exclusively on the front-lines. So, ratcheting up the background checks was step one.

The next phase was to look at incorporating integrity tests and biodata assessments into the selection process, as well. Integrity tests can really help organizations discover behavioral tendencies toward the unethical — and they are also well-validated instruments and legally defensible as part of a robust selection process.[1]

Biodata assessments ask questions of applicants about their life history and experiences. These assessments have also been validated to reveal propensities toward unethical behavior. Using both of these tools will help this organization to increase the quality of individuals that they hire, and do so in a relatively cost-effective manner. We then recommended to the task force that they leverage Human Resources even more to examine the local labor pools, and potentially overhaul their local recruitment strategies. Obviously, if we can improve the source, we can improve the outcome.

Finally, we spoke about the need to change the organization's culture at the senior-leadership level and at the front-line-manager level to focus on hiring individuals with integrity rather than just becoming efficient at bringing in people to work. The typical costs of firing are high enough, but now, adding in the extreme costs associated with product shrink, the combined costs were having a definite material impact on the organization's future.

Impacting Critical Employee Attitudes

Employee attitudes will always play an important role in achieving any business outcome, and this organization's outcome of product shrink was no exception. Customer Focus was a key factor from their employee opinion survey that also was revealed by the analysis to have a strong impact.

The employee attitude of Customer Focus was measured by the following survey items:

- "Customers depend on me for service/product needs."
- "I understand that what I do impacts the customer experience."
- "I have high standards for how customers are treated."

Recommendation #5
- Focus on Job-Person Match to Focus on the Customer

Focusing on the customer is important, but it is not 100 percent clear, from a tactical perspective, how to have a direct impact on employees' Customer Focus. Our first recommendation was for senior leaders and front-line managers to constantly and consistently link any directive and initiatives to the way in which they will positively impact the customer's experience. Connecting the dots from employees to customers, rather than just giving out orders, is a key opportunity for individuals to see how what they do on a regular basis has an impact on the business. In addition, from the analysis, you have the ability to go a step upstream and find what factors/attitudes are driving Customer Focus. We discovered, in this organization, that Job-Person Match was a key driving force behind getting employees to focus on the customer.

Job-Person Match was defined as employees (1) getting a sense of personal accomplishment out of their work and (2) actually looking forward to coming to work. This makes practical sense, as well, because if people do not get much from their jobs and also don't want to punch-in, they probably are not going to go out of their way to help the customer and, in this case, it showed. Based on this information, we first recommended that realistic job previews be incorporated into the selection process. Front-line positions in this organization are considered relatively low-skilled jobs and, honestly, are not extremely exciting either. That aside, individuals who apply for jobs should know what they are getting into — warts and all. This will help applicants to make an informed decision about whether or not to accept the position, and it can help you to not bear the costs of a short-term hire. Most importantly, it will directly impact your overall Customer Focus — which is a key driver of product shrink.

Next, we recommended incorporating job rotations for front-line employees. There can be a certain level of monotony to entry-level jobs, and this rotation would help keep interest up. It will also have the added benefit of yielding a cross-trained workforce. Allowing people to move around will show them that you are investing in them, and they will reward you by focusing more on the customer while effectively executing their jobs.

Finally, we recommended that employees' job descriptions be expanded, particularly for those with strong potential. Allowing employees to participate in other areas beyond their day-to-day jobs will improve their desire to come into work every day and also give them that sense of personal accomplishment that was identified as critical on the employee-opinion survey.

Based on the analysis shown previously in Figure 3.3, we would prioritize our focus as follows:

1. Improving the Achieving Outstanding Results Competency.
2. Ethics Course Participation & Sales/Product-Shrink Course Participation.
3. Reducing Dishonesty Terminations.
4. Improving Employee Attitudes of Customer Focus and Job-Person Match.

II
Demonstrating the Value

This section will take you through key issues for all organizations (sales, productivity, and turnover) and demonstrate, with case studies, how the Business Partner RoadMap™ is implemented in different organizations (displaying the success that it has had). The payoff is a detailed overview of how to discover the key drivers of business outcomes, implement effective initiatives, overcome obstacles, and show the financial impact that HR has on these key issues.

CHAPTER 4

Increasing Sales Revenue

Organizations continuously look for new sources of revenue to meet stakeholder expectations of growth, increased market share, or their own expectations for financial outcomes. Therefore, tapping into new sales channels or lead sources is always appealing. Of course, revenue generation begins with the sales function within an organization, but it doesn't have to end there. There are a myriad of untapped human resources (invisible levers) within organizations that could, and should, be mobilized to generate sales for the company. Many organizations have not yet come to the realization that they can turn their entire workforce into "part-time account executives." There are thousands of potential customers who are not focused on and possibly lost forever, because of a completely underutilized resource — the company workforce. Thousands of non-sales employees, who have thousands of contacts outside of the organization, are going untapped because their company does not promote sales activity outside of the sales department. Just two examples of this could be instituting a referral program or expanding job responsibilities of existing client-facing employees. Companies experiment with these initiatives on a daily basis, with mixed results. What is the role of Human Resources in discovering and maximizing this invisible lever, and how can the employee data be used to assist this process?

Human Resources has a two-fold role in this capacity. First, Human Resources will play its more traditional role in helping with tasks such as job-design or referral incentives. Second, and most importantly (because it is rarely done in most organizations), Human Resources can leverage its wide variety of employee data to understand drivers of employee referrals/sales conversion rates. To do this, Human Resources must, of course, gain access to the referral/sales data for the target employee population. That information enables Human Resources to determine what drives employees to turn in sales opportunities and, further, how they can use that information to improve the operating units that are not getting their employees to participate and sustain the performance of those units that are getting results from their people. This is truly the great potential that exists when you break down data silos and connect employee data to real business outcomes.

The lead-generation data (on its own) is a great tracking tool to allow you to see where the organization currently stands and to track progress, but it does not tell you why the results are the way they are, nor does it tell you what you need to do in order to impact and improve those results. It is simply a scorecard. At the same time, HR data around employee opinions, competencies, training, and employment tenure, etc., is also a "nice to have" on its own. It can give great insights into the work environment and the overall abilities of the organization. However, employee engagement, job satisfaction, or great leadership competencies are not business outcomes. These data have the sole purpose of being *drivers* of business outcomes. Meanwhile, very few organizations are using these data to demonstrate how they are driving business outcomes and determining where investments should be made to reach those outcomes.

Bringing together the business development leaders and Human Resources to discuss connecting their data for the good of the company (in this case, revenue generation), is critical for competitive advantage. This, as we will show you in the case study of a large company, does reap substantial financial rewards for the organization.

Tracking Lead Generation

Setting up a program and platform in which employees can provide sales opportunities — and in which the organization can track and sell those sales opportunities — is not difficult; in fact, we have worked with organizations that have been quite successful with it. As with any sales department, the tracking of sales opportunities is essential to proper discovery, proposing, and closing of sales, as well as managing the sales workforce to harvest the opportunities. This tracking mechanism needs to be extended to all employees in the workforce. Creating opportunities for all individuals in your organization, so that they may have the skills and motivation to go out and promote your products and services to their network of contacts, means generation of more sales opportunities.

Tracking the Data

For multiple reasons, the key to tracking lead generation is to collect that data at the operating-unit level and at the individual level. First, we recognize that not all of your people-related data will be tracked at the individual level. For example, you will want to keep your employee-opinion data anonymous, thereby making tracking individual survey responses back to exact individuals impossible. However, lead-generation data should be linked back to exact individuals to recognize them for performance. Thus, you will need to "roll-up" the individual results to the operating-unit level because that should match the level at which you capture your employee-survey data. Second, organizational cultures are based on individuals working together in a group and managed by a single manager. Tracking the lead-generation data at the operating-work unit (basically, the data for an individual manager's group) is critical to making that linkage to the opinion-survey data for the manager's group as well. Consolidating this data into one spreadsheet and using a standard statistical software package are the key steps needed to conduct a meaningful analysis that links aspects of the work environment (the opinion data), to the relevant business outcome (the lead-generation data). The ability to use data, such as employee-opinion data that your organization already collects, and connect it to relevant business outcomes (in this case, lead generation) is the essence of working across data silos. Breaking down and connecting the data silos is the solution that will enable Human Resources to graduate from practitioners in the personnel department to leaders held accountable for the company's business outcomes.

Principle 6: The organization's data exist in silos.

The Sales Opportunity

Employees who dip into their well of associates, contacts, friends, and relatives to promote your company's products and services will put a smile on any leader's face. The fact that individuals in your workforce took time "off-the-clock" to generate business for the organization, with nominal or zero direct financial reward to themselves, makes this act exceptional. But it begs the question, why would your employees do this? What are the motivating forces, management behaviors, or key aspects of the workplace environment that would drive an individual to want to work off-the-clock for the benefit of the organization? We have asked numerous business leaders, and here are the more common answers:

- "It's no surprise to me; we have the best people in the world here at XY Corporation."
- "Our people are committed to our mission statement and that is what motivates them."
- "Our brand is so strong that XY people are attached to it and it permeates their lives."
- "Who wouldn't they want to help their own company make more money? It's a win-win situation as far as I'm concerned."

That last one makes sense in that employees might see the connection between making the company more money and ultimately making themselves more money. But it is difficult to create that type of line-of-sight for many employees outside of the sales department. What you probably notice about these leaders' answers is that they really are not based on facts or analyses, but on intuition and optimism. This becomes dangerous. As different work units begin to slide in the number of sales opportunities they are generating from employees, more money will be invested in the types of things that the executives *think* are driving the reduction in sales opportunities.

Principle 7: There will be obstacles and barriers to obtaining the data
(e.g., politics, turf battles).

A key assumption from executives is that activities such as communicating more about the lead-generation program, using more media, and having relaunch parties around the organization will get the sales numbers to rise. In many cases, the numbers will rise temporarily. However, this activity will result in a vicious cycle of peaks and valleys in the generation of sales opportunities without any sustained improvements in lead generation or long-term performance. There is, quite frankly, too much money at stake to put a key aspect of competitive advantage in the hands of a feel-good tactic like a pizza party. All the while, two key data silos (Sales and Human Resources) are like two ships passing in the night — with little or no data collaboration, which ultimately results in no additional revenue for the organization.

Theoretical Backing

From a theoretical and academic perspective, the idea of going above and beyond the employee's specified job duties has been well documented and defined as an "organizational citizenship behavior" (OCB). Dennis Organ originally conceptualized OCBs as behaviors that were intended to benefit an organization's mission, but were not directly related to one's prescribed job duties.[1] However, the underlying notion of OCBs is that they were behaviors that occurred within the proverbial "walls" of the organization. It is great to know that the idea of employees helping out other employees continues to be studied, and that academics have discovered various aspects of a person's personality that would drive their desire to be a good organizational citizen. This again underlines our point that it is often difficult to put a dollar figure on this concept because this type of data is tied up in the HR function.

Do organizations (besides heavily unionized organizations) actually have exact job descriptions anymore, where individuals could truly go "above and beyond" and be measured objectively on their actions? What would drive employees to want to go out of their way for their organization? It is a critical question that must be answered and it is one that gives Human Resources an opportunity to have an immediate and tangible impact on the revenue that is brought in by the sales function. The case study in the next chapter will shed light on how to follow our process with great success.

CHAPTER 5

Increasing Sales Revenue:
A Case Study

The senior leadership team at a *Fortune* 500 organization saw their new sales dipping. While the balance sheet was strong, the sales group knew an opportunity existed to implement an Employee Sales Generation (ESG) process, in which individual employees could turn in sales opportunities for the organization's products/services.

The program was launched with great fanfare, with the CEO leading a large kickoff rally at the company's corporate headquarters. Training sessions followed to teach employees what constituted good sales opportunities and what did not. Initial participation and interest in the program was high; nominal prizes were even given to individuals who turned in "hot" opportunities.

Competitions started springing up between different departments to see who could turn in the most sales opportunities in a month, and "number of sales opportunities" even began appearing on many managers' performance plans. You know where this story is going. Roughly six months into the launch, excitement had waned and motivation slipped. Worse still, managers with "number of sales opportunities" on their performance plans began pressuring their employees to turn in sales opportunities. Of course, the quality of those sales opportunities was weak, and the sales team suffered terribly by chasing dead sales opportunities instead of managing their quality accounts or going after quality sales opportunities. Ten months later, the program was stagnant, a mere afterthought for employees, who really could not see a connection between turning in sales opportunities and, well, anything. Other than some nominal reward, there really was not a bigger reason to go out (on their personal time, no less) and find high-quality sales opportunities. And, finally, the pressure put on employees by their managers to turn in leads caused rifts.

The sales group was certainly not just sitting on their hands. They had spreadsheets full of data from the program to sift through and pore over, and they made some modest discoveries. Different geographically organized work units showed great disparity in the amount and quality of the sales opportunities that were turned in by employees. Knowing that the incentive to turn in sales opportunities, although limited, was *identical* across all work units, the sales group's assumption was that the probable cause of the disparity was the quality of local leadership. They glanced at the data and then took a look at which leaders were lagging behind, and it looked like the "usual suspects," according to the corporate sales function. Based on this "analysis" of the data by the sales group in their function, they set out to re-educate many of the local managers who fell below a certain threshold of "number of sales opportunities" generated. The sales group desperately tried to reinvigorate the program by reiterating its importance, and re-explaining how to find good sales opportunities. The local managers wanted to help. They wanted to get their people to turn in more sales opportunities. Their hearts were in the right place and once they had been retrained on the ESG process, their minds were in the right place as well.

A few months went by and, not surprisingly, the sales-opportunity numbers did not move much. The sales group leaders were frustrated and at a loss to explain why their attempt at reinvigorating the program had failed.

Unfortunately, as the sales group was toiling away with their limited data in *their* own function (tracking the sales opportunities by geographic unit), the HR group was busy focusing on their own data (e.g., internal HR efficiencies and compiling and reporting annual employee survey data in *their* own function). So while these two groups worked in their own areas and kept their data separate in their respective functions, their organization's top-line was suffering.

This is a situation that many organizations find themselves in and, unfortunately, they do not even realize that they are "in" it. This was an excellent opportunity for senior HR leadership to throw their hand up in a meeting and offer to assist the sales group — and, that is exactly what they did. As the plug on the program was about to get pulled, we also stepped in and partnered with this organization to help solve their problem.

To reiterate, our process for breaking down data silos consists of six critical phases (repeated in Figure 5.1).

Phase 1: Determine Critical Outcomes

Unfortunately, it is often the case that systems have to break down or outcomes have to underwhelm before our process is implemented. Our stakeholder interviews with senior leaders revealed that this employee ESG program was high on the CEO's strategic initiatives list at the beginning of the fiscal year — December. This was one of numerous strategic initiatives on the organization's plate, as we discovered during the stakeholder interviews. This was not a problem as our process is designed to focus on numerous business outcomes simultaneously to make the time spent as productive as possible. (We provide a sample stakeholder interview guide in the Appendices for your use.) While we discovered that this

Figure 5.1 The Business Partner RoadMap™

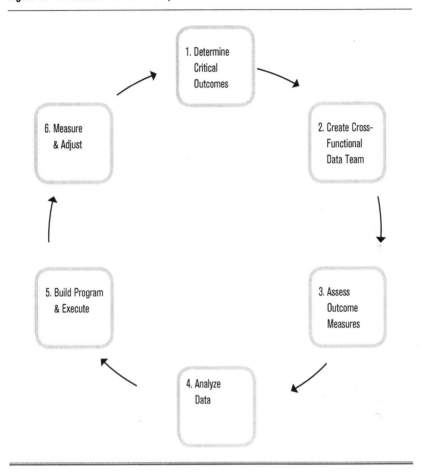

particular sales program had been in place for more than a year, let us be clear: It is really never too late to implement this process. The data will be there and the outcomes — if critical to the business — can be salvaged.

As is often the case, the metrics that senior leadership tied to this program were relatively straightforward. Success for this program, in the eyes of senior leadership, was assessed by (1) the number of employee sales opportunities generated, (2) the percent of employee sales opportunities sold (conversion rate), and (3) the revenue generated from employee sales opportunities. These metrics were on the organization's balanced scorecard. This information is the springboard to launch the process. To quote Stephen Covey, "Begin with the end in mind"[1] or in this case, "Begin with the business outcome in mind."

Phase 2: Create the Cross-Functional Data Team

The next key phase is to partner with the senior leadership team member who has ultimate responsibility for the business outcome that you are going to examine. In this case, it was the senior vice president of sales, and we needed him to appoint an individual from the sales group who had access to and knew how to manipulate the sales-opportunity data. That individual became the sales representative on the Cross-Functional Data Team (CFDT). Following our recommendation on how to structure these data teams, a representative from every other major function in the organization joined the team, as they all had strategic initiatives that could be supported and enhanced by Human Resources.

At our CFDT launch meeting, we covered the following agenda:

- Goals of the team
- Advantages/positive outcomes of participation
- Discussion of linkage process
- Demonstration of a typical business-outcome linkage project
- Strategic initiative review
- Balanced scorecard review
- Critical sub-metrics for the balanced scorecard
- Next steps
    - » Prioritize projects.
    - » Schedule follow-up meetings with data owners.

The goal of this meeting is not to merely assign tasks to other functions. Our approach is different because (1) we take the opportunity to gain buy-in as to why we are doing what we are doing and (2) we want those data owners to feel comfortable with turning over their data to someone outside of their own function for analysis. (Turning over data is a key obstacle that we discuss later.) This obstacle was mitigated by our launch meeting when we ended up spending a substantial amount of time conducting an informal Q&A session, putting the team representatives' minds at ease. This allowed them to be involved in the analysis to the extent that they preferred and, of course, co-present the results to the senior team, if desired.

In this case, the result of the initial CFDT meeting was to assign the sales-data representative to gather the relevant data together and have a follow-up meeting with our analysis team.

The Follow-up Meeting

The follow-up meeting was the next logical step, because we really got into the granular details with that team member: how the data is collected, when it is collected, at what level within the organization it is collected, and what type of data is captured besides the necessary pieces (e.g., employee demographics). In this case, we discovered that, in addition to the necessary sales information, data on individual employees was also captured. These data, such as length of service, department, and past performance are all important data to examine when looking at why something is happening — or in this case, not happening.

Phase 3: Assess Measures of Critical Outcomes

We mentioned earlier that the key measures of success for the program were: (1) the number of employee sales opportunities generated, (2) the percent of employee sales opportunities sold, and (3) revenue generated from employee sales opportunities. This was great information to have, but the data needed to be collected with two key components — frequency, and the level at which the data are collected — taken into account.

Frequency is important because it makes intuitive sense that, when looking to make the necessary cause/effect assessments, you must establish a logical, chronological connection in the data. In this case, employee-opinion data was collected before the outcome of sales-opportunity data was collected; and the sales data was collected on a monthly basis, whereas the employee-opinion data was collected on an annual basis, in July. From the frequency, we developed our data-analysis strategy. We decided to use the employee-opinion data from July and the sales data from the six month period from August to January. This strategy allowed us to have employee-opinion data that was collected *before* the sales data was collected.

Level of Data Collection

When collecting data, it is critical to match the data levels. Rather than get into too detailed of a discussion on statistics, suffice is to say that we need to compare "apples to apples." In this study, the level at which the sales data was collected (the work-unit level), needed to match the level at which the employee-opinion data was collected (also the work-unit level). Had these two levels not matched, the data would have needed to be aggregated to a level that matched. This can complicate the analysis. Our analysis team had accumulated the necessary sales data and employee-opinion data for all of the work groups in the organization, and was now ready for the next phase.

Phase 4: Analyze Data

There is a need to demonstrate more than just an overall correlation between employee opinions and sales opportunity metrics. Unfortunately, many ROI gurus will say that a correlation demonstrates some sort of cause/effect relationship, which is not true. It further relegates Human Resources down the food chain, as senior leaders need more than a weak correlation as evidence to make a large capital investment.

This approach allowed us to make the necessary cause/effect inferences from the sales opportunity and employee-opinion data. Our analysis revealed that three key areas were having a significant and cause-and-effect impact on the sales opportunity metrics (see Figure 5.2). The key areas were as follows:

■ Management communication skills

■ Work/life balance, stress

■ Lack of understanding of the company strategy

Figure 5.2 Sales Impact Framework

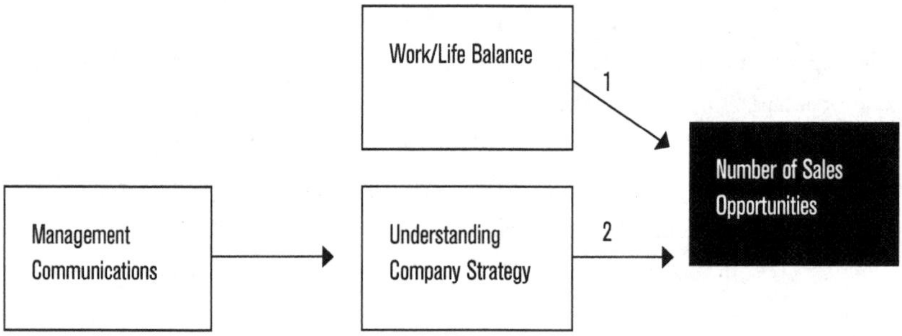

This analysis was a far cry from what you typically see when it comes to statistical analysis of business data. Having evidence that indicated three key management areas were significantly impacting sales opportunities was obviously better than saying "happier employees will turn in more opportunities" or "better leaders get better results." Using this linkage analysis, the organization was able to identify the specific drivers of sales opportunities from the multitude of potential drivers (e.g., regard for employees, pay, and benefits). This sales group now had specific, actionable areas upon which to focus to get the sales-opportunity program back on track. Even better, they had an as-of-yet under-utilized partner in Human Resources to help them reach their goals.

Gaining Senior Leadership Buy-in

At the completion of the analysis, we reconvened the CFDT to share all of the results that we had discovered. At this meeting, we created a strategy to present the results of the analyses at the next sales-leadership meeting, in order to gain buy-in on the initiatives that needed to be put into practice, based on the results of the study. It was decided that our analysis team, a senior HR leader, and the sales-data representative would lead that presentation. After gaining sales leadership buy-in, the next step was to gain buy-in from the senior executives (the C-Suite). To gain buy-in, the analysis team and the senior vice president of sales (along with the other senior leaders represented on the CFDTs) presented findings and proposed solutions at the monthly senior-executive meeting. Gaining buy-in and, more importantly, funding, was less problematic for the team because we had the data and the business case to back up our request.

Phase 5: Build Program and Execute

It is important to remind you that although Phase 5 is extremely important in the entire process, we will not go into great detail because we are not here to advocate a specific silver bullet. Your organization and its culture are likely to have very little in common with the organization in this case study. It is dependent upon your organization's leadership to use *your* data to determine the invisible levers that exist in *your* organization.

We could just as easily have called this phase "*Co*-Build and Execute," because we advocate that as a particular course of action. In this example's organization, success was more probable because the sales group partnered with Human Resources to build the programs that would allow the key causal drivers that emerged from the analysis (management communication skills, work/life balance, and understanding of company strategy), to be instilled in the organization's DNA. Human Resources and sales conducted focus groups and targeted surveys with front-line employees and discovered critical areas in which to improve work/life balance. In this case, it wasn't necessarily more days off that appealed to the workforce, it was merely more flexibility in the work schedules. Plus, employees were quick to point out that there was not any motivation to work off-the-clock or add more work to their own plates, when they already did not get to spend enough time with their families. Human Resources invested in better scheduling software and training, on not only how to maximize the benefits of the scheduling software, but also the benefits of allowing employees to have more control over their own schedules.

Those brief targeted surveys and focus groups reinforced the fact that the lack of understanding of company strategy was directly linked to the poor communication skills of the managers. Yes, it makes intuitive sense, but employees could not get on board with going out of their way to find sales opportunities when they did not know why they should. If you recall, the sales group determined that employees were not on board because local management was not pushing it hard enough. The data said otherwise, and the invisible levers were uncovered. So, front-line managers got customized communications training that was co-built by our team. This same group co-built an initiative to communicate company strategy and results, including weekly updates for employees on the local units' financial performance, and quarterly briefings on company performance and company strategy. There was also a monthly update on the sales-opportunity results and recognition for strong performers.

Phase 6: Measure and Adjust

Data analysis is not a one-time event and should never be treated as such. First, those who discovered the invisible levers now have a new or expanded level of accountability for the sales-opportunity program results. The opportunity to measure the ROI of their new, co-built programs was a must. We calculated the ROI in the following manner:

Revenue generated from employee-generated sales opportunities in the six months leading up to the launch of the new initiatives was $28 million. In the six months following the launch of the new initiatives, the revenue generated was $39.76 million — a revenue increase of 42 percent. The investments in the initiatives totaled $3.6 million ... ($39.76M-$28M)/$3.6M = 326.6 percent ROI.

The analysis continues. Instead of resting on their ROI numbers, Sales and Human Resources conducted the analyses again with their most recent data. The re-analysis revealed that employee recognition was emerging as an invisible lever that could be pulled; just knowing about the company strategy and how the program worked was a vast improvement. The follow-up focus groups revealed that the newly energized employees wanted a piece of the action, if the sales opportunity that they turned in actually got sold. As prescribed, re-analysis — as new data is available — is a continuing critical step in the process and the continuing success of your business.

Takeaways for Human Resources

These three invisible levers (work schedule flexibility, management communication skills, and company strategy updates) were not getting pulled, and the sales opportunity program stagnated. For more than a year, the data existed in two separate functions, just waiting to be analyzed. Of course, it was being analyzed, independently, which is not nearly as effective and certainly has less of a chance of having an impact on the organization's bottom line. Suddenly, following the implementation of the initiatives, the sales team was delivering results and Human Resources could now definitively say that they not only had a hand in it, but they could also quantify just how much of an impact they had.

The takeaways for Human Resources are to:

1. Get out of its own function, look beyond its own department, and simply improving its own efficiency metrics;
2. Link cross-functional data and work with leaders across functions;
3. Properly analyze cross-functional data;
4. Discover causal drivers of the business outcome;
5. Attack and enhance the causal drivers; and
6. Demonstrate the business impact and ROI of enhancing the causal drivers.

Now the HR group at this organization has a staunch ally in the sales function and respect as a player at the table — with the recommendation of the senior vice president of sales, of course. Plus, when the HR professionals at this organization look at the annual report, they will no longer see themselves only on the cost side of the balance sheet.

CHAPTER 6

Powering Productivity

Due to the exceptional work of Kaplan and Norton in *The Balanced Scorecard*,[1] nearly every organization uses a balanced scorecard. What makes the balanced scorecard great is that it does just what it says it's going to do — it keeps score and (if crafted correctly) is balanced across financial, customer, and internal operations, and people metrics. In many cases, this has created the need for each function in the organization to then have its own balanced scorecard, with another slew of metrics on which to set goals. Again, the balanced scorecard does what it says it's going to do, which is to keep score.

Perpetuating the Silo Mentality

Many, if not all, of the functions mentioned or listed above only focus on their own metrics — and rightfully so — because all functions have enough to do without worrying about those metrics that they believe they don't have any impact on or for which they are not held accountable. This, unfortunately, perpetuates the silo mentality and, even worse, keeps the myriad of data collected for all of these scorecards in their own silos as well.

Principle 6: The organization's data exist in silos.

This begs the following question: If we spend so much of our time just trying to collect data in order to keep score, when do we actually start examining things cross-functionally to improve the scores? The HR function has perfected this science of just keeping score — never stopping to think about how the metrics link together and where the invisible levers are which can be pulled.

The balanced-scorecard data is typically available to all managers within an organization. This means that the data are free to be analyzed and connected to other data outside of the functional silo. Undoubtedly, there is more than one cause of a balanced-scorecard metric and, better yet, there is more than one area of the business that can have an impact on that metric. The HR function is in a great position to have a strong impact on the balanced scorecard because they are involved with, and have people data across, *every area of the organization.*

Focusing on the Scorecard Data

When establishing CFDTs, it is important to make the balanced scorecard the centerpiece of your initial meetings, as this data has already been deemed critical to the organization by senior leadership and should be treated as such. Furthermore, there is no better or easier way to show an immediate impact from your teams than to demonstrate the invisible levers to pull that are relevant to balanced-scorecard metrics. One caution to keep in mind is to first focus on the individual functions' balanced scorecards and not the broad, organizational balanced-scorecard metrics.

Those broad organizational-level metrics are the sum of the efforts of many functions/people, and trying to show strong direct impacts of employee data — measured at the work-unit level — on broad organization-level data, may be a stretch that you do not wish to make just yet. Think about the Sears employee-customer-profit chain study referred to in Chapter 1.[2] It showed very high-level linkages across employee attitudes, customer attitudes, and business outcomes. Ultimately, the study concluded that minor shifts in employee attitudes would have massive revenue increases. That is a little bit of a stretch, plus the study did not drill down to show what aspects of employee attitudes to focus on, nor did it account for the fact that more than just employee attitudes alone have an impact on customer attitudes. "Think globally, act locally" is a phrase that might be relevant here. Remember, we did not focus on the connection between total sales and overall employee attitudes in Chapter 5. We focused on a key aspect/program that is designed to impact total sales. In the long run, this will provide the opportunity to more precisely quantify the impact that Human Resources has had on a specific business outcome.

Productivity metrics normally make up a high percentage of an organization's balanced-scorecard metrics, and rightfully so, as organizations need to focus on the bottom line as much as they focus on the top-line, whether they are a rapidly growing or mature business. Most managers are continuously thinking about how to get more productivity out of their people. Of course, some tactics are more effective than others, ranging from team barbecues to reward plans. Also, with some managers, you have history working against you ("That's the only thing that works around here, and it has worked for 50 years"). Of course, you may even be working against a not-so-relevant list of excuses about why productivity hasn't increased — from the lousy weather to the poor magazines in the break room to the ever-present "lack of staffing" argument. With the Business Partner RoadMap™, the question becomes, "How can you connect employee data to productivity metrics and identify invisible levers?" This is a great opportunity to put the CFDT into action.

Stakeholders

As mentioned in Chapter 2, are HR leaders and the various heads of operations having in-depth discussions about how Human Resources can improve productivity beyond compensation, rewards programs, or filling position requisitions? More than likely, critical business decisions are being made on assumptions and history, rather than on reliable data and analytics. Key stakeholders for productivity will include the senior leadership in the organization.

As mentioned, the productivity data are being collected at the operation work-unit level for the balanced scorecard. Meanwhile, Human Resources will have employee data at that level as well, including staffing numbers, turnover data, opinion-survey data, training-course data, individual performance appraisal ratings, and demographic data. All these data have the potential to be invisible levers that can be executed to increase balanced-scorecard metrics. Part of what makes the CFDT exciting, is that besides identifying causal drivers, it can also confirm or dispel key myths within the organization (like the ever-present, "We aren't fully staffed" argument).

CHAPTER 7

Powering Productivity: A Case Study

A *Fortune* 500 company was struggling with improving its efficiencies. History was working against it, because as new ideas to fix the issues were bubbling to the surface, they were just as quickly being discredited with the "If it ain't broke, don't fix it" argument. Innovation is never easy, but attempting it in a top-down bureaucratic organization can be nearly impossible. It becomes even more difficult if there is little hard evidence to support changing "the way we've always done things around here." Risk aversion is tough enough to overcome, and is nearly impossible without any data to back up your ideas and assertions.

As with any consultation, when we took on this organization as a client, our goal was not to prove that the powerful old guard's approach was broken or wrong, but rather to show, through the organization's own data, that there were powerful invisible levers that were important and that could be incorporated into their classic approach to operating their business (and if we could use data to debunk some old theories, then so be it).

Phase 1: Determine Critical Outcomes

Now you might be thinking to yourself, "If the balanced scorecard is already created and the metrics set, why do you even have to go through Phase 1?" Even though the metrics have already been set, conducting the key stakeholder interviews will help identify the few, most critical metrics. Second, balanced-scorecard metrics are weighted differently. Frankly, some are more important than others. This is where our case study suddenly becomes two-pronged — and with good reason. After conducting stakeholder interviews with the CEO, COO, and the senior management in operations, finance, and Human Resources, it became obvious that revenue and profit were the company's two most important balanced-scorecard outcomes, and the rest of the 23 metrics were drivers of those two outcomes. Fair enough. But we weren't just going to *assume* that the remaining metrics had an equal impact on revenue and profit. We realized that a critical need for the CFDT that was about to be formed was to first use the structural-equation modeling technique to determine which of the metrics would emerge as significant invisible levers to pull in order to impact revenue/profit. After making that determination, then we could look at the specific data that would impact those balanced-scorecard metrics that were truly important to the "real" bottom line (revenue and profit).

Phase 2: Create the Cross-Functional Data Team

At this particular organization, operations (as is typical) not only had accountability for the balanced scorecard, but they also captured and housed all of the data. We convinced the COO to appoint the balanced-scorecard manager to the CFDT. This was critical because it opened us up to all of the people and functions who provided the manager with the data used to create the scorecard. Remember, the balanced scorecard cuts across the entire organization, so having the individuals who are responsible for capturing the balanced-scorecard data from each function participating on the CFDT was quite useful.

Phase 3: Assess Measures of Critical Outcomes

If you remember from the Increasing Sales Revenue Case Study (Chapter 5), the two key components that are imperative to assess are the frequency and level at which the data are collected. This was not a difficult obstacle for this particular analysis, because all of the data on the balanced scorecard were captured at the same frequency (monthly) and at the same level (the operational work unit). However, we needed to first determine which of the "other" 23 metrics, that were not profit or revenue, had a significant impact on those two outcomes. The good news (and it should be this way in your organization) was that we had access to the balanced-scorecard metrics for the previous three years.

Phase 4: Analyze Data

The same process that we used in the Driving Sales Case Study was also appropriate to incorporate to analyze the balanced-scorecard data. Again, this was a two-pronged approach. First, we analyzed the data to determine which of the 23 operations metrics had the biggest impact on profit/revenue. This analysis revealed that numerous balanced-scorecard metrics were important to profit/revenue, but on the operations side, "time-to-produce" and "errors-per-customer" were the two key metrics that were shown to be the strongest causal drivers of profit and revenue. Time-to-produce measured the time that the product began its cycle in operations until it was ready for the customer. Errors-per-customer measured the effectiveness at which every geographic work unit got the customer the right product within the agreed-upon time frame. The benefit of this exercise was to narrow down the 23 operations-focused metrics into a manageable list on which to focus. Further, this initial analysis showed us that nine of those other operations metrics weren't having much of an impact on profit/revenue (we like to call that "bonus information").

Now that we had two critical operational metrics to analyze, we then needed to examine what, from a people perspective, were the invisible levers that could be pulled to impact "time-to-produce" and "errors-per-customer." We had plenty of people data to examine, from staffing levels and employee opinions to (surprisingly) number of poor weather days. Once again, we used our statistical methodology of choice, and staffing was not a significant invisible lever to pull that impacted productivity; this debunked some of the history that was working against the organization's forward progress. Actually, the analyses revealed that knowledge of the local work unit's service goals, and how well they performed versus those goals, were the most significant causal drivers of the productivity metrics. Training quantity and quality, along with work/life balance, were the other significant invisible levers that could be pulled to impact productivity. We put those invisible levers in Figure 7.1.

Figure 7.1 Productivity Framework

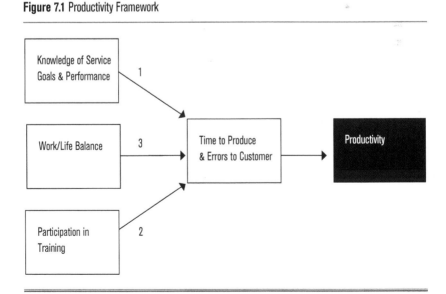

Phase 5: Build Program and Execute

The data tell a convincing story about how to impact productivity, and, as we helped this organization build strong initiatives around the invisible levers, the anecdotes that we heard from front-line employees put quite an exclamation point on the data. We heard from employees that they had never heard of a "balanced scorecard." They basically told us that if there was yelling from management, it meant that they must not have hit their numbers for that particular time period, and if they didn't hear anything that must have meant that they hit their goal. Not such a pleasant and motivating work environment, is it? Furthermore, work/life balance programs were laughed at by employees because local managers would not "let" employees use them. Training classes, which would have helped employees to do their jobs more productively, were also discouraged by front-line management because they felt those classes took their people away from work and this, from their perspective, negatively impacted productivity.

To rectify the situation, middle management went on a "road show" with our data analysis to show front-line managers around the world that focusing on the three key invisible levers would truly help them to increase their productivity. They then stressed that help would be on the way shortly in the form of tools and initiatives to make the invisible levers a reality.

We then got involved and helped the senior stakeholders build the key invisible-lever programs. First, we realized via follow-up discussions and brief surveys with front-line operations employees that work/life balance did not necessarily mean more paid-time-off, it really just meant an ability to swap shifts every once in a while with fellow employees. This program's goal was to give employees an intranet-based method of adding flexibility to the shifts that they worked. Employees, a few days ahead of time, could swap shifts with co-workers and get done what needed to get done in their personal lives. This was a 24-hour-a-day company, so shifts, and employees willing to swap, were plentiful. Human Resources took the reins on this program.

Next, front-line managers made it a point to post their daily goals, as well as the work unit's performance vs. those goals. Now, yelling and silence were no longer the methods of communicating goal achievement. Friendly competitions sprung up between different shifts, and numerous opportunities for recognition/rewards became apparent to managers. This was a relatively simple solution to a lingering problem.

When the front-line managers began to buy-in to the invisible levers and the data behind them, because of the two initiatives above, the organization made a large investment to upgrade its training programs and their availability. Due to the resulting productivity improvements, attendance at training courses, and the willingness of front-line managers to take employees off the floor to attend the training courses, has increased significantly.

Phase 6: Measure and Adjust

When we discussed the "front-line manager's view" earlier, we noted that front-line managers ultimately care first about how they are doing against their own balanced-scorecard metrics, and that if you cannot help them perform on those metrics, well, good luck. Now we do not say this to disparage these managers, but rather we say it to those corporate functions that have made a career out of adding many less-than-useful activities to the front-line managers' plates. It's not difficult to imagine how well a work/life balance/new training/service goal presentation would have gone over with front-line managers without any real data to back up their usefulness. This goes on everyday in organizations around the world. In fact, this organization had tried to pilot test some work/life balance programs in the past and hit brick wall after brick wall in the form of front-line manager pushback. Now this organization had data to get these programs implemented and, therefore, bought into. But the ROI is what matters.

The first productivity metric that we went after was "time-to-produce," and the overall organizational performance in the six months leading up to the launch of the new initiatives was 6.2 hours. In the six months following the launch of the new initiatives, the "time-to-produce" fell to 5.6 hours — an improvement of 9.67 percent. The second metric was "errors-per-customer delivery." In the six months leading up to the launch of the new initiatives, this was 0.09 (meaning an average of 0.09 errors per 100 products produced). In the six months following the launch of the new initiatives, errors-per-customer delivery fell to 0.06 — an improvement of 33 percent! The organization knew what the costs per efficiency improvement and the costs of a customer claim meant to the organization. The improvements saved the organization $81 million dollars annualized in the first year that the initiatives were put into place. The investments in these initiatives totaled $6.2 million dollars. Our analysis showed that the productivity metrics had a 0.19 impact (beta weight) on profits. If we take 19 percent of the $81 million dollars, that yields $15.39 million in impact attributed to the initiatives: $15,390,000/$6,200,000 = 248 percent ROI.

Armed with our process of discovering invisible levers, this organization found just how much of an impact these levers could have on their balanced-scorecard metrics and their "real" bottom line (profits/revenues). Human Resources can lay claim to a substantial piece of the $81 million in savings.

Principle 8: Once a connection/linkage is made with the data, accountability is unavoidable (and that's a good thing).

Human Resources should be happy with its newly discovered bottom-line impact, but they now have newly discovered metrics on the balanced scorecard on which they will be held accountable by the CEO — and we aren't talking about internal HR-efficiency metrics. Knowledge equals responsibility. The point is, as HR leaders demonstrate the impact of people on business outcomes, they must also be prepared for a new level of accountability that comes with the demonstration of increased value.

CHAPTER 8

Decreasing Turnover

HR departments have a good idea about the various costs associated with turnover and communicate those costs relatively well. The costs include recruitment time, interviewing time, ramp-up time, and training time. Once again, though, Human Resources is only communicating the costs and impacts of turnover on, you guessed it, Human Resources. Are we to think that the CEO of an organization is going to put an investment in turnover reduction at the top of his or her monthly meeting agenda based on recruitment time spent to replenish those positions? Of course not.

There are many key causes and downstream impacts of the turnover situation in any organization that need to be uncovered through analysis. A short list of turnover causes that academics have researched, and that we have found in our own analyses, includes: aspects of the work environment,[1] employee characteristics/personality traits/demographics,[2] overall unemployment rate,[3] pay,[4] leadership style,[5] and line of sight between performance and rewards.[6] From our work with small and large organizations, we have seen key downstream impacts of high turnover, including: reduced customer satisfaction, productivity losses, reduced profitability, and HR costs. However, when it comes time to attack the turnover problem, the business case is rarely comprised of the upstream causes or downstream impacts of turnover with data to back up the arguments. It is no surprise that demonstrating these causes and impacts is a task that is rarely undertaken in many of the best organizations — the statistical methodology is not a simple one. This is still particularly frustrating because many of the data that are needed to demonstrate the causes of turnover and its impacts are housed within the HR function. For many, it is just easier to say that turnover is bad and we should reduce it. Everyone can agree with that, but evidence as to how to fix it, or its true costs, remain elusive.

Some Research on Turnover

If you examine the research that exists on turnover, the consensus of opinion is that job satisfaction and organizational commitment are the two most consistent aspects of the work experience that are connected to turnover or an individual's intention to turnover.[7] The issue with a good portion of academic research, in general, is that, on a practical level, it does not tell organizational leaders what to specifically work on to address the turnover problem. Merely concluding that satisfaction with the job and commitment to the organization are important to reducing turnover does little to help the HR manager or front-line manager who is struggling to have a real-life impact on turnover. This is why it is up to your CFDT to examine the data that exist in your organization, discover the invisible levers to pull, and reveal the key downstream impacts of turnover.

Theories of Turnover

When considering a complicated business outcome such as turnover, it is important to place it in a proper framework for the discussion. A fully-agreed-upon theory would be a great place to start. Unfortunately, there is not a widely-agreed-upon theory as to why people leave organizations. But that shouldn't discourage us, because there are plenty of good ones out there to use if you need to. One example is Social Exchange Theory,[8] another is Perceived Organizational Support (POS),[9] and still another is Job Embeddedness Theory.[10] There are many more turnover theories, but we will only briefly look at these three as this is a book about action and not theory.

Social Exchange Theory focuses on the notion that a relationship between two people is maintained by person "A's" behavior reinforcing "B's" behavior, and person "B's" subsequent behavior reciprocating the original behavior from person "A."[11]

POS has been explained as: "the magnitude of support employees expect of the organization shown through fair pay, praise, approval, and concern for making the job interesting and meaningful which would be rightfully exchanged for effort, high performance, commitment to, and retention in the organization."[12]

Job Embeddedness Theory encompasses the connections that people have to other teams, groups and people (links), perceptions of fit with the organization, community and the job (fit), and what the person would sacrifice by leaving the job/organization (sacrifice).[13] What makes Job Embeddedness Theory unique is that it attempts to capture the myriad reasons why individuals *stay* with the organization rather than why they leave. The theory accomplishes this by categorizing these components of retention into the three distinct areas of the work experience discussed above: links, fit, and sacrifice.

One theory is not likely to be "better" than another, and there is no one best theory. However, if you use a framework that fits best with your organizational culture, and create opinion surveys and analyze data from that standpoint, you will have an advantage in communicating the results and driving change.

The ultimate drawback with these theoretical frameworks is that they try to paint everyone or every organization with the same brush. This is, of course, at odds with the entire premise of this book. What we want you to do is discover a framework that best fits the culture in your organization. Analyzing your own data and uncovering why your specific employees are leaving the organization is far more important than attempting to apply, or possibly trying to prove, a broad-based theory.

Putting Theory into Action

Having a personalized theory around to discuss turnover issues is always important because it can help you to create a strategic framework for how you are going to attack your own turnover problem. But, unfortunately, theories have little practical value if they are not tested within the context of individual organizations using data specific to their employees. We also know that organizations tend to take a limited perspective when collecting and analyzing data as it pertains to turnover. It is important to take a look at how most organizations attempt to collect data from their employees concerning turnover. Below is a short, but not exhaustive, list of the most popular turnover data strategies.

Exit Interviews

First, exit interviews have been used for years and are now standard operating procedure for most organizations. In fact, it would probably feel a little strange for an employee to leave a job without getting a standard exit interview, either online, on paper, or one-on-one with a representative from Human Resources. One of the problems with an exit interview is that, well, the horse has already left the barn (your employee has already quit). It is too late to suddenly start asking employees for their perceptions, opinions, and suggestions about the work environment (assuming, at a minimum, that opinion surveys are not being conducted). That said, exit interviews do supply some useful information, but they certainly should not be the only time that information regarding your work environment is collected from your employees. Another issue with exit interviews lies in the fact that companies administer them to all employees who voluntarily leave. Sure, you want to be fair, but some of those employees who are leaving you may actually *want* to leave. They could be severe under-performers, problem-causers, complaint-filers, or those that just don't fit into the organizational culture. What happens with most exit interviews is that all of the data, whether it is quantitative or qualitative, is placed into one big database. So the strong-performers' data are thrown in with the under-performers' data and both are given equal weight. You really want to know why your *best* people are leaving the organization and you may not necessarily put too much stock in the reasons why those folks who have been ineffective for years are leaving.

The Monthly/Quarterly Turnover Report

The second typical approach is the monthly or quarterly (depending on company size) employee-turnover report. We are sure that you are probably spending too much time, money, and effort on creating these reports. They have little value above being slightly informative. Do a quick internal assessment and you will discover that multiple individuals spend multiple business days dedicated to sending out these turnover reports by a certain arbitrary day of the month. You probably realize that we are pretty darn accurate in our assessment. At least we hope that we didn't *under*estimate the time you are spending. Now, do another quick assessment and compute the value that the organization is deriving from these reports. These reports suffer from the same issues as exit interviews — the people have already left the organization and we have now decided to look at some data about turnover. *Autopsies are informative, but you cannot test new medicines on cadavers.* Yes, there are a wealth of data in these turnover reports that could be analyzed, but are you taking advantage of it? For example, have you looked at pockets of strong-performer turnover with certain managers? There is good information in those reports, but it is likely going unnoticed in the intense flurry of effort to get the tracking reports sent out across the organization.

The Organization-wide Turnover Metric

The third approach that is widely used is setting an organization-wide turnover goal. This can be a great motivator for all levels of management that shines a light on the critical problem of turnover. It is also used to set aggressive goals for turnover reduction for which all managers can be held accountable. This approach, too, leaves a lot to be desired. First, most HR leaders do not reveal the invisible levers that need to be pulled in order to impact turnover. Thus, a balanced-scorecard metric/goal is not a silver bullet to solving the turnover issue, and it may actually promote the wrong or ineffective behaviors. In many of the organizations we work with, we discover that a turnover balanced-scorecard metric is met with great fanfare. However, front-line managers in those organizations revealed to us that they became more gun-shy about firing sub-standard employees because, well, they "wanted to hit their balanced-scorecard goal for turnover." This, of course, has the "vicious cycle" effect of letting poor performers off the hook while, at the same time, strong performers see that sub-standard work goes unaccounted for; and this potentially motivates the strong performers to look elsewhere for employment. With analysis and discovery of the organizations' invisible levers existing within the turnover data, you will be able to discover why the best people are leaving and hold the organization accountable to a stronger high-performer turnover metric.

To be clear, a turnover balanced-scorecard metric should be part of a healthy retention program, but it should not be implemented on its own and without proper analysis of exactly (1) what type of turnover is most critical to the success of the organization, (2) what is causing turnover in the organization, and (3) what are the key pockets of turnover that you should place your focus. Only a process of discovering key aspects of the company strategy, and an in-depth data-analysis approach, can tell you that.

A more robust approach to turnover should include the following elements:

1.   Linking employee-opinion data to actual turnover data to discover why employees may leave (or stay).
2.   Interviewing strong performers who have left the organization.
3.   Linking employee turnover to business outcomes.

This approach will add to the credibility of Human Resources because it will help you to discover why the best employees are leaving, prevent valued employees from leaving in the future, and how that impacts the overall business.

Employee Opinion Data to Actual Turnover. It really is a shame, but many organizations spend hundreds of thousands of dollars (or more) every year to conduct census-wide employee-opinion surveys. These organizations look at their strengths and weaknesses, conduct focus groups, create some action plans, and set an improvement goal for next year's survey score. Of course, you should do those things, but that is not nearly enough. You only get one proverbial "bite at the apple" to collect this rich data from your employees. Yet, many organizations do not take full advantage of the data that are collected because they do not conduct anything more than a few weak correlational analyses (if any at all) between overall employee satisfaction and profits. The approach that should be taken does include (1) work-unit-level reports, (2) opinion scores on annual performance goals, (3) specific action-planning, and (4) systemic reports and goals. But the key opportunity to take advantage of is the discovery of the invisible levers that will show why current employees stay with the organization and why strong-performing employees have left. Figure 8.1 gives you a visual breakdown between a generic "linkage" analysis, and our thorough approach to discovering invisible levers. Approach #1 shows a correlation between overall employee satisfaction and overall turnover. This is useful to know, so that you can say that employee attitudes matter when it comes to turnover.

Figure 8.1 A Generic and a Robust Linkage Model

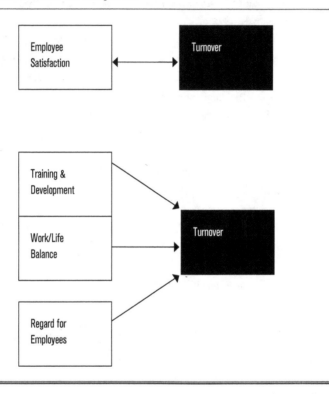

However, approach #2 will not only tell you that there is a connection between employee attitudes and turnover, it will tell you specifically which attitudes are causing employees to turnover. Furthermore, notice the arrows connecting the boxes. This correlation just means that the two constructs are related, but does not identify which construct causes/predicts the other. Using the traditional example from your intro statistics course, shark attacks and ice cream sales are highly correlated, which just means that both increase during warmer months. So, you don't expect one to cause another, as a different reason explains their relationship. The second approach can actually identify a causal relationship between data. From a practical standpoint, this means that by changing one variable, you can change the related variable. In an organizational setting, making decisions based on causal relationships is the only thing that makes sense.

Principle 9: Don't assume a link between employee data and business outcomes — define it and understand why or why not.

Conduct Follow-up Exit Interviews with Strong Performers. To reiterate an earlier point, exit interviews on the last day of employment have their flaws, chief among them that you are getting opinions from strong performers *and* under-performers — when you really want to know, specifically, what the strong performers think. Another opportunity exists to follow-up with your strong performers after they have left your organization, by conducting a post-exit interview over the phone, about 60-90 days after they have left. Critical invisible levers exist here as well. First, the insights into the work environment that your strong performers can provide are extremely valuable. Second, in our experience, strong-performer feedback during a post-exit interview rarely matches the data that are collected during the traditional exit interview process. This typically occurs because strong performers in particular will not be inclined to burn bridges with overly candid feedback about individual managers or the organization as a whole. The time away from the organization will give them some perspective and put them in a safer environment to speak candidly. Third, as a bonus, you have the opportunity to re-recruit strong performers back into your organization because they may have discovered that the grass is not truly greener on the other side.

As you can see, not all of the data you need to collect is going to be quantitative. The richness of the qualitative data from strong performers makes it critical to solving the turnover puzzle. Telling the story that your data will reveal is the next critical step in the process.

Telling the Integrated Story. The myriad types of data that exist in your organization must be brought together to be analyzed. The same is true for the critical aspects of the overall employment experience that impact turnover. These data must be not only collected, but also analyzed, to discover the invisible levers which are causing your turnover. These data, in one place, tell quite a compelling story from how employees view the organization, what drives them to potentially leave, and why your best employees walked out the door. Only looking at the exit-interview data on the last day of employment leaves the invisible levers undiscovered.

The story you tell with the data should flow as follows:

1. The organization's rate of turnover, with specific focus on your strong-performer turnover numbers.

2. The specific job-types that have the highest levels of overall turnover and the highest levels of strong-performer turnover.

3. Based on the causal analysis, display the key employee attitudes, from the employee-opinion survey, that are driving people to potentially leave the organization.

4. Based on a qualitative analysis, display the key reasons why your strong performers have left the organization. Be sure to also display the names of the strong performers who you have interviewed, as this will have a strong impact on the executives in the audience.

5. The causal analysis will show how much of an impact employee attitudes have on turnover (the business case), while the qualitative data will enhance the analytics.

6. These results will drive the creation of your organization's action plan to attack turnover. That plan is the subject of the next chapter.

CHAPTER 9

Finding Root Causes and Solving Turnover: A Case Study

It has always been somewhat straightforward for academics and researchers to theorize about why people leave organizations. As cited in the previous chapter, academic research indicates that job satisfaction and organizational commitment make people less likely to leave your organization. That's nice to know, but how does a manager specifically create organizational commitment or job satisfaction? Remember, the academic evidence is certainly nice to have, and it looks good in a presentation at corporate headquarters, but how do we put it into action out in the operations? It is a different story when it comes to identifying why people leave, and *then* making substantial financial and time investments based on those findings, to get results.

A large retail organization was having problems with their part-time turnover rate. This is not a surprise, as many retail organizations suffer from high turnover on the front-lines, and many leaders in this industry have just accepted that this is the "way it is." Various estimates of average annual turnover in retail organizations are anywhere from 60 percent to more than 100 percent. Many retailers have just trained their leaders to be skilled at making fast hiring decisions and incorporating high turnover into their plans rather than discovering and tackling the root causes of the turnover problem. Well, we aren't ones to throw in the towel that easily, and, thankfully, neither was the organization we worked with. The organization's leadership had taken many of the typical steps that are normally done by leadership to ascertain the reasons for excessive turnover. Exit interviews were administered (on the last day of employment) to every employee leaving the organization. Monthly turnover reports were created by the HR function (which took three full-time employees and 10 business days to create, by the way). They conducted employee-opinion surveys once every two to three years and examined the high and low scores. Not surprisingly, compensation scores on the survey came back low, and poor manager/employee relations were also an issue. To remedy this, senior leadership slightly increased the starting pay rate for part-timers and accelerated the overall pay-increase time frames. They also spent more than a million dollars to hire a training firm to come in and train their managers on how to create better employee relations, particularly with part-time employees. They threw resources (HR people and money) at locations with low-scoring employee relations survey items. Next, senior leadership created a target turnover metric that was included on the balanced scorecard, and held all managers accountable to (try to) reach the number.

As you might expect, the organization did not gain much traction with these actions, the turnover rate remained high (from 72 percent to 103 percent, with an average of 86 percent), and the stores that were especially weak at retaining people at the start of all of this remained especially weak. Incredibly, this organization lost and hired 8,600 part-time employees per year, at an hourly pay rate of $7.00/hr.

Initial Impressions

We spoke with the CEO and the Senior Vice President of Human Resources, and they felt that they had done what they could to impact turnover and stated flatly that this is "typical for our industry — and that's what we benchmark against."

We were concerned that exit interviews on the last day of employment were the only consistent measure used to gather data on turnover. We, of course, mentioned that the "horse has already left the barn" when it comes to conducting exit interviews, and that individuals tend to be less than truthful because they do not want to burn any bridges on their way out the door. We discussed further that conducting employee-opinion surveys erratically (every two to three years) rather than annually, was limiting their impact. Our focus when meeting with the CEO and Senior Vice President of Human Resources was not solely focused on the results of their data collections, but rather on their process. The process for collecting the data is critical — and the results and root causes will be what the data say they are (and not what they are assumed to be).

Phase 1: Determine Critical Outcomes

Using our stakeholder-interview process (see Appendices), we met with the CEO, COO, Senior Vice President of Human Resources, CFO, and CIO to determine the critical outcomes on which we needed to focus. Not surprisingly, some of these leaders thought that they had the whole turnover problem figured out. When we asked the question, "Do you know what drives people to stay or leave this organization?," their typical answer was, "well, obviously its compensation and manager/employee relations, because they are our lowest-scoring opinion-survey items."

What is important to note here is that these senior leaders, with our urging, came to the realization that only reducing part-time turnover numbers was not, necessarily, the critical outcome the organization needed to be successful. After interviewing these senior leaders individually and as a group, the decision was reached to focus on reducing high-performing part-time turnover. The dark side of aiming for an overall reduced turnover metric is that, in many cases, turnover can be a good thing — if low performers are the individuals turning over. The CFO recognized not only the costs of hiring, but also the much higher costs of keeping low performers. These senior leaders also noted that a critical outcome that *might* be causing part-time turnover included front-line manager turnover. This was an important piece of information as it was based on an assumption, but it gave us an opportunity to test the credence of their theory. It is also important to note that we discovered many other important business outcomes on which to focus — and we recommend that you do the same. However, for the purposes of this chapter, we will focus on turnover.

Phase 2: Create the Cross-Functional Data Team

The next important step in our approach with this organization was to put together the CFDT. The "data representatives" were individuals from Human Resources, Finance, Operations, and Customer Service. As usual, the key to an effective CFDT is to have executive support. To that end, the Senior Vice President of Human Resources, the CFO, the COO, and the Vice President of Customer Service kicked off the meeting, to not only show support, but also to remind the team of the critical nature of the work they were about to do. The flow of these meetings was to discuss the ultimate reason for the meeting which, in this case, was to discover the root causes and business-outcome impacts of turnover across the organization. The first step was to establish the business case for reducing turnover. To accomplish this, we needed to bring together the data that the organization used to measure the performance of their stores. The second step was to determine the root causes of turnover, which was accomplished by gathering the data that existed across the entire employment experience — the organization regularly measured training, development activities, management behaviors, performance, employee opinions, and exited employees' opinions.

Phase 3: Assess Measures of Critical Outcomes

Like most organizations, multiple metrics were used to measure performance, including:

- Customer-satisfaction ratings
- Profit margins
- Revenue

- Costs
- Part-time turnover
- Dollars per customer or "share of wallet"

Employee data also was captured, somewhat sporadically, including:
- Training participation
- Employee opinion
- Exit interviews

Phase 4: Analyze Data

There are two steps that need to be followed to make sure that the data is ready to be analyzed: (1) making sure that all of the data is measured at the same level (i.e., the store level) and (2) analyzing data that makes sense in terms of timing. This meant that we had to have, in chronological order, the most recent employee opinion data and then the most recent turnover and accompanying demographic data. Basically, we were looking at the turnover data that occurred after the employee-opinion data was collected. It makes little sense to connect last year's turnover numbers to this year's employee-opinion data (unfortunately, those people are long gone and wouldn't have participated in the survey).

It is important to make sure that your employee-opinion survey includes items that assess the full gamut of your working environment, i.e. content validity. This is vital to conducting a strong analysis. Thankfully, this retail organization had done a nice job by using a well-validated survey instrument.

Figure 9.1 details the items from the opinion survey and the specific items that are causal drivers of part-time turnover.

Phase 5: Build Program and Execute

The results of the analysis showed that four key areas of the work environment were invisible levers within the organization that should be pulled to reduce part-time employee turnover. The first three invisible levers were from the organization's employee-opinion survey, and the fourth key driver was front-line manager turnover. The first invisible lever was part-time employees' perceptions of their benefits compared to other employers in the area. The second invisible lever was the part-time employees' perceptions of the company's involvement in the community. The third lever was the part-time employees' perceptions of the spirit of teamwork that existed in the stores. The fourth and final lever was the level of front-line manager turnover on an annual basis across all stores. This was great

Figure 9.1 Turnover Impact Chart

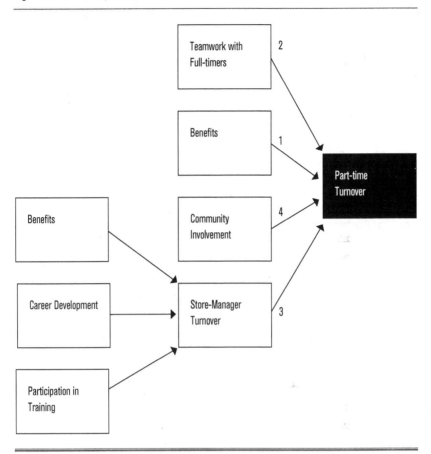

information to know, and there were a lot of actionable items now available for both executives and front-line managers. Let's take each invisible lever one at a time.

Employees' Perceptions of Benefits. Taken at face value, your first reaction might be, "Well this is just like people complaining about compensation, another problem that needs money thrown at it." That is a fair reaction, but after presenting the results and speaking with HR leaders, front-line managers, and even part-time employees, this was not a problem of the quality of the benefits package. The realization was that this organization did a poor job of promoting the quality of its benefits package. The surprising truth was that this organization had one of the best benefits packages for part-time employees in the area, but they did not do an exceptional job of letting their people know about it. Leaders had also neglected to "sell" the benefits package to potential part-time employees during the recruitment phase. So, rather than adding to their cost-basis with lucrative upgrades to the benefits plan, they added a relatively small amount to a better communication strategy of the benefits plan to current and future part-time employees.

Teamwork. This was an interesting key causal driver of part-time turnover, as the prevailing wisdom regarding part-time employees is that they are there to work during school or for a short amount of time and may not be as committed to the organization as full-time employees. This organization quickly realized that since they assumed part-timers were not overly committed or just there for extra pocket money, that's exactly how the managers treated this critical part of the workforce. This lackluster attitude from management is what came across loud and clear to part-time employees — and, of course, it was a self-fulfilling prophecy. Follow-up focus groups and analysis showed that part-time employees wanted to be a part of the team, amongst fellow part-time employees, and viewed as true teammates with the full-time employees as well. The organization invested in team-building exercises that placed part-timers and full-timers together, and they also invested in management skills training that focused on how to manage a part-time workforce and how to assimilate them into the culture of the organization in the same manner as full-time employees.

Community Involvement. This is another interesting area which generally receives attention for public relations purposes as well as to demonstrate corporate responsibility/sustainability. However, it is not typically thought of as a key causal driver of part-time turnover. Again, this is why the data should drive the HR strategy, rather than conventional wisdom. It turned out that the part-time workforce at this organization had a high interest in the level of volunteer activities that were sanctioned in the local community. The obvious investment here was to create opportunities for employees to give back to the community and then to better communicate to employees about the financial contributions that the organization typically made throughout the year. There was also a renewed effort to incorporate the organization's community involvement activities during the recruiting phase as well.

Front-Line Manager Turnover. As we looked beyond the employee opinion survey, we discovered that front-line manager turnover was a key driver of not only part-time turnover, but also direct financial outcomes as well. We noted that the organization had all but given up on part-time turnover; however they had not spent a substantial amount of time on full-time turnover because they were ahead of the benchmark. This organization came in at 32 percent front-line manager turnover, with their benchmark coming in at 40 percent turnover. By looking solely at norms and not conducting any analyses in their own organizations, senior leadership had accepted someone else's standard and missed an opportunity (this is why they are called *invisible* levers).

To battle this issue, we conducted another analysis because we needed to know the key drivers of front-line manager turnover. What we discovered were three key causal drivers that included: (1) perceptions of benefits, (2) actual training opportunities completed, and (3) perceptions of long-term career-development opportunities.

The first invisible lever — benefits perceptions — works well because it is consistent with the part-time employee driver. The approach to having an impact was making sure that the benefits plan, and how competitive it is in the marketplace, were focused on all employees and not just towards part-time employees. Obviously, the front-line manager benefit plan had more options and was more lucrative in certain areas, so the messaging was modified to reflect that information.

The second invisible lever was centered about the front-line managers' participation in important training and development courses offered by the organization. In follow-up interviews and focus group meetings, we discovered that managers were turning over, or threatening to turn over, if their upper-level managers did not take any interest in their development. This manifested itself in their awareness of the trainings that were available and, of course, their ability to get permission from their bosses to participate. This lack of proactively training front-line managers was a key lever of turnover. We helped the organization build out a training plan, which would not only get front-line managers participating in the training, but also would have their bosses get involved in the process and take an active interest in improving front-line manager development. The key here was that the organization had tracked the data on front-line manager training, but had never put it into a context of impacting business outcomes.

The third invisible lever was the front-line managers' perceptions of their long-term career-development opportunities in the organization, as measured on the employee-opinion survey. This certainly coincides with the training (or lack thereof) of the front-line managers as their desire to move up, learn new things, and take on new challenges was a driver of their desire to stay with the organization. Two key initiatives were implemented to take on these issues. The first focused on creating a series of defined career-path possibilities. Front-line managers were made aware of the types of experiences, training, and education that would be needed, based on the type of career progression in which they would be most interested. To be clear, the career paths did not start with the front-line manager position, but started with entry-level positions and first focused on how to become a front-line manager and from there, how to move on to a position of higher authority, for example, an area manager, or how to move into a functional or support position. The second initiative to build upon the career-pathing initiative was for area managers (who managed front-line managers) to actively have open and honest discussions with front-line managers regarding career-development opportunities on an annual basis, at a minimum. The defined career paths were great, but they would not have been effective without a plan for communicating them to the people who needed to be aware of them — the front-line managers.

Phase 6: Measure and Adjust

The leaders in this organization took action and used these analyses and created a solid, analytics-based strategy and initiatives. The temptation amongst many leaders, normally, is to implement these initiatives, make them permanent, and assume that this will solve the turnover problem forever. However, the world and our work environments change constantly, so wise leaders will do two things: (1) create strong metrics to make sure these initiatives get executed effectively, with leaders held accountable and (2) create a culture of measurement where progress is tracked and these analyses are replicated annually to discover any potential new drivers of part-time employee turnover (and other business outcomes). Keep in mind that the organization, as a whole, must constantly re-analyze the competitive landscape, internal capabilities, etc., and adjust the company strategy as needed. Our point is that the organization does not keep the same strategy year after year — so why should Human Resources?

This organization created metrics and goals for the entire organization around the key invisible levers impacting part-time turnover. They were:

1. Significant improvement in part-time employee perceptions of the benefits plan on their now annual employee-opinion survey.
2. Significant improvement in perceptions of teamwork on the employee-opinion survey for part-time employees.
3. (a) Significant improvement in perceptions of the organization's involvement in the community, as measured on the employee-opinion survey.
   (b) A 100 percent increase in the amount of company-sanctioned volunteer activities. All front-line managers and HR managers were held accountable to this metric.

The fourth invisible lever was front-line manager turnover. As noted, this was a driver of part-time employee turnover, but it also was an "outcome" in and of itself, which necessitated more analysis to discover what was driving front-line manager turnover. For the invisible levers discovered in the analysis above, the metrics that were created to impact front-line manager turnover included:

1. Significant improvement in front-line manager perceptions of the benefits plan on the annual employee-opinion survey;
2. 100 percent completion of all mandatory, introductory front-line manager training courses;
3. 100 percent completion of all advanced front-line manager training courses for all front-line managers identified as high performers and/or high potentials;
4. Area managers complete 100 percent of career discussions for front-line managers, including a checklist-based discussion of career-path opportunities; and
5. 100 percent of high performers and/or high potentials having at least one developmental assignment (promotion or lateral development move) in the past 18 months.

Human Resources also included metrics on the execution, and completion, of the initiatives described above. For example, these metrics were focused on (1) developing the career discussion guides for area managers and training all area managers on its effective use; (2) facilitating the developmental moves for the high performers and high potentials; and (3) effectively delivering the training courses completed by the front-line managers.

The results of the strategic initiative implemented across the organization were impressive. Part-time turnover dropped from an average of 86 percent in the previous year to 38 percent in the following year. This represents a 55.8 percent decrease in part-time turnover. If we use the conservative statistic, that it costs 25 percent of an annual part-time employee's salary to replace the employee, then the original cost of this turnover on an annual basis was $15.05 million (calculation based on 1,000 hours worked per year at $7.00/hr, on a total of 8,600 turnovers; with 25 percent of that number being the final "cost" of turnover). A 55.8 percent decrease yields a cost of turnover in the current year of $6.65 million. That is a decrease of $8.4 million. The organization spent $2.5 million on the initiatives reviewed above — yielding an ROI of 336 percent for tackling part-time employee turnover, which is impressive.

Again, front-line manager turnover was not only a driver of part-time employee turnover, it was also an outcome (and an important issue!) in and of itself. The organization was suffering from a 32 percent turnover rate amongst front-line managers, just in the previous year. The current year, after the initiatives were implemented, yielded a front-line manager turnover rate of 21 percent. The organization lost and hired 185 front-line managers in the previous year. This total cost of turnover was $4.625 million (calculated using a conservative cost of turnover of one half of the front-line manager's average salary of $50,000). The current turnover rate of 21 percent represents a 34.3 percent decrease in front-line manager turnover. The current cost of turnover now stands at $3.05 million, which now saves the organization $1.575 million in the total cost of turnover. These interventions, in sum, yielded a savings of $9.975 million. On a total investment of $2.5 million, this yields a total ROI of 399 percent.

CHAPTER 10

Driving Results: A Case Study for Small-to-Medium-Sized Organizations

We realize that a fair share of the examples given in this book focus on larger organizations, particularly the *Fortune* 500. Of course, we have applied this process successfully in numerous organizations with fewer than 4,000 employees and below $100 million in revenue. The great news is that the process of the Business Partner RoadMap™ is identical (and equally effective) no matter what the size of the organization. However, the data analyses can be slightly different. To that end, a case study will illuminate the process in a small- or medium-sized organization, with emphasis on the differences in its applications.

Organizational Overview

The organization had 490 employees, with just over $75 million in revenue in the previous year, and was focused in the service industry. They were not a public company and were not necessarily surviving day-to-day; however, their culture focused on having employees "work like you are trying to keep the lights on." They were struggling in many areas (as we discovered from the stakeholder interviews we conducted). Because they were a small business, a large team of HR representatives was nowhere to be found. It was apparent that their three HR employees wanted to know how they could directly impact the bottom line to help the company "keep the lights on" (but weren't 100 percent sure of how to go about doing it).

Phase 1: Determine Critical Outcomes

The stakeholder interviews are largely the same with smaller businesses, as their leadership structures are relatively similar, and the issues those leaders face are just as daunting (e.g., profit margins, cash flow, revenue, turnover, customer satisfaction, etc.). After conducting stakeholder interviews with the CEO, CFO, Senior Vice President of Human Resources, and Senior Vice President of Sales, the most critical issues facing the organization were (1) consistent front-line manager performance, (2) employee productivity, and (3) customer satisfaction. These interviews yielded an outcome that concerned us — a paralyzing fear that proper measurement was not possible for these areas of concern because "the service industry is not as exact as the manufacturing industry." It is, of course, possible to measure properly in the service industry, which we will talk about next.

The leaders were optimistic, good-natured, and did not believe in detailed performance evaluations. They believed that if the numbers turned out OK at the end of the year, then everyone must have done their job. Fair enough. These stakeholders did note that data was being collected on individual performance, and there were key data to determine business outcomes for every manager in the organization (e.g., sales figures, account growth, customer satisfaction, and individual performance). We also discovered that turnover was below three percent, which is a strong number, and not something we would forget, because we were headed down the path of greater accountability — which might impact turnover in the future.

Phase 2: Create the Cross-Functional Data Team

This relatively small organization did collect much of the data around which they had severe concerns (manager performance, productivity, and customer satisfaction). However, they had a tendency to aggregate that data to the organization level rather than also looking at the individual level or the work-unit level to truly hold people accountable for the results. The CFDT consisted of representatives from (1) sales, (2) Human Resources, and (3) information systems. In an organization of this size, this covered what was needed to retrieve the necessary data.

The CEO kicked off the meeting, surrounded by the entire executive team (this is an advantage of working with a smaller organization). She spoke of the need to focus the organization on collecting data at the work-unit level, for accountability, but also the importance of working to discover what drove individuals to reach those all-important numbers. This was certainly a "sea change" for this organization that formerly had a family-oriented approach to management lacking in accountability. This also set a strong tone for the data team, as they knew this was an important element of business and a new direction for the company.

This organization worked exclusively in the United States. The country was split up amongst 48 managers, who each ran a geographic district. These managers were responsible for all operations in their district, as they were each run as a P&L. This was good news of course, as the data collected for the overall district included: total sales, customer retention, account growth, customer satisfaction, on-time product delivery percentage, and profit margin. Individual productivity metrics included total sales per representative, customer satisfaction, and on-time product delivery percentage.

Phase 3: Assess Measures of Critical Outcomes

From the HR perspective, we had employee data that was also collected at the district level. This data included: (1) employee demographic data (e.g., length of service, time in position, education level), (2) employee-opinion survey data, and (3) employee-training data. The HR data (the predictor data) was collected at the same level as the critical-outcomes data. This made for a smoother analysis as we did not have to aggregate any data to a higher level.

Phase 4: Analyze the Data

The key to the analysis is lining up the data. To that end, we integrated the data and lined up the predictor data with the corresponding outcome data. What we were looking to discover were the key causal drivers of the critical outcomes. Figures 10.1, 10.2, and 10.3 show the key drivers of each of the critical outcomes. When examining all of the invisible levers, you will also notice the considerable amount of overlap amongst the levers across the key outcomes. Across these analyses, four key areas were shown to be invisible levers for all three of the critical business outcomes. Those levers for all employees were:

1. Sales Training Completion
2. Employee Recognition
3. Co-worker Relations

Figure 10.1 Sales Impact Model

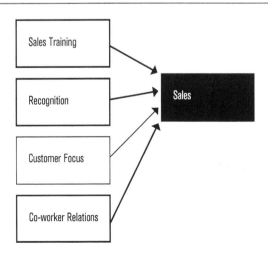

Figure 10.2 Customer Satisfaction Impact Model

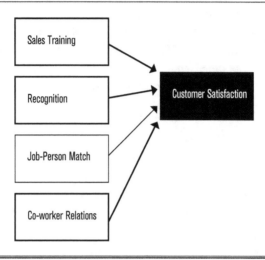

Figure 10.3 Profit Margin Impact Model

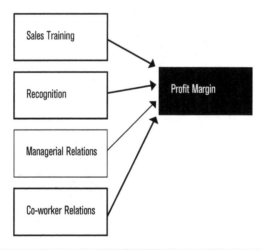

Phase 5: Build Program and Execute

In small businesses, the approach, analysis, and synthesis of the data is identical to larger entities. The difference lies in the sheer quantity of data available to analyze — and, sometimes, less is more. For this organization, they had only required those employees who worked exclusively in sales to complete an extensive array of training courses that focused on sales and customer-service skills. It was apparent that, across the 48 geographic operating areas, these courses were a key causal driver of all three critical outcomes of sales, customer satisfaction, and profit margin.

Our first step was to make the sales-training courses mandatory for all employees. The modeling showed us that the impact was 0.22, which is a statistically significant value and showed a potentially strong ROI would be achieved by acting on this invisible lever. The beta value is the number that shows the strength of the relationship between variables.

Second, employee recognition was a key invisible lever. To give some context to the situation, this was a family-oriented culture that tried to reward everyone the same way, if the company was successful. The cliché is to call this the "peanut-butter" approach to management, which spreads everything around evenly. On paper, it makes sense, but reality tells us a different story. So, quotas were set for sales employees to motivate them to strive for achievement, while non-sales employees were given an opportunity to set goals for customer-satisfaction scores and for new products/services created. In this way, employees could be recognized for individual achievements as well as the achievements of the collective organization.

The third invisible lever that we discovered was focused on co-worker relations within the operating districts. Some context will help explain this particular area of focus. As an organization that still had a very strong "founding" family influence, those employees who were a part of the early days of the organization felt that they were in "rarified air." This sense of being there from the early days gave these individuals a strong sense of entitlement, which, of course, was the root of a significant amount of friction in many work units — especially with newer employees who were not present for the grand opening. The analysis gave credence to this prevailing theory, and the CEO/founder admitted to being in denial about this issue until the data gave her undeniable proof. Team-building exercises were implemented but, more importantly, the new focus on measuring manager performance, and holding managers accountable for their performance (based on objective data) quickly put an end to any perceptions of favoritism. Objective metrics for performance for all employees eliminated any lasting effects of entitlement. According to our follow-up interviews with employees, this entitlement attitude was common knowledge amongst the people on the front line, but it was not until it proved to be a drag on business outcomes that senior leadership stepped up, took notice, and took action. This was a key learning moment for the HR leaders in this organization, as they had found a strong tool to create change within and across the business.

Phase 6: Measure and Adjust

Calculating the ROI of initiatives and interventions is always the best way for HR professionals to show their value. This, of course, does not change no matter how large or small the organization. Value can be shown because (1) you will have proof that what you did had, and will continue to have, a direct and causal impact on key business outcomes; and (2) with this causal proof, showing ROI will not be a grasping-at-straws scenario, but a true exercise in demonstrating the financial impact of your actions. Again, this matters in organizations of all sizes.

Total sales in the previous year's first two quarters, before the launch of the new initiatives (sales training, co-worker relations, and employee recognition), was $42 million. In the current year's two quarters, following the launch of the new initiatives, total sales generated was $53.62 million — a sales increase of 27.67 percent.

The investments in the initiatives totaled $1.34 million. The ROI was calculated using the following formula:

New Total Sales − Previous Total Sales/Investment Amount in Initiatives = ROI
or
($53.62-$42M)/$1.34M = 867 percent ROI

The analysis showed an average impact of 0.23 for the invisible levers. Twenty-three percent of the 867 percent ROI yields an HR impact of 199 percent ROI. Not bad. In that same time period, profit margins also increased by 13 percent, and customer satisfaction scores (as measured in "percent favorable") increased by 11 percent. Human Resources has made a strong and, more importantly, *provable* impact on this organization's critical business outcomes.

After a year had passed and the initiatives had been implemented, we replicated our analyses using the new employee-opinion survey data, as well as the training and demographic data. We do this because as invisible levers are pulled and issues are rectified, new areas of concerns and new invisible levers may manifest themselves as the organization continues to evolve. This is a critical step in the process as Human Resources doesn't just have to show value one time, they must constantly show their value with strong analytics. According to the most recent analyses, in fact, new invisible levers had manifested themselves, and the HR leaders are currently well on their way to establishing a transformation that includes consistent measurement and analysis that guides all of their work.

Getting It Done

The realities of the day-to-day job and the obstacles that HR leaders face in the organization will present a potentially long road to success. This section is designed to give you the tools and skills to work through key issues/obstacles such as (1) getting data from other departments, (2) pulling multiple pieces of data together to tell a compelling story, (3) creating metrics to drive accountability, (4) front-line manager pushback, and (5) examining external business challenges.

CHAPTER 11

Breaking Down Data Silos to Drive Results

There are plenty of business books available that theorize about flattening organizations and eliminating silos.[1] We are not here to put forth another argument against silos or put forth new theories about how organizations "could" look. Most organizations had, currently have, and will continue to have an organizational structure that is in separate functions. It is a fact of life — and in many ways it is an effective way to organize work — but rather than discuss the pros and cons of various types of organizational structure, we want to offer you solutions to work within, and be successful, in an organization of silos. An advantage of the organizational hierarchy is that all departments and functions are subjected to the same hierarchy. At a minimum, you at least know where to find people, as their function is clearly defined. It may sound odd, but this type of consistency can be a saving grace when attempting to create your CFDTs. As will be shown, it will not be easy, but it is OK to embrace that structured organizational chart and hierarchy. Plus, the process that we have shown you in this book will be your ticket to building relationships with other departments and functions (by helping them to reach their goals by doing your job in Human Resources); in other words, "breaking down silos!"

Organizational charts do not create silos, the people who confine themselves to those little boxes do.

The key to obtaining any other department's data lies in demonstrating opportunity. The opportunity is to discover what specific aspects of your people data can help that other department's leaders to be more effective. We should also call this a business case.

The Sales Approach — The Value Proposition

Assume the role of a salesperson. First, you need to blueprint the client to discover what their needs are and where you can help. Instead of asking for all of their data all at once and then leaving, you need to find out the strategic initiatives that are top of mind to the leader. Then you will need to figure out the specific metrics that are tied to that initiative. You will probably need to look no further then the balanced scorecard. Finally, figure out the metrics that make the most sense to be tied to people metrics, such as the work environment or competencies.

That senior leader that you approach, who has just begun working on these key initiatives and is now accountable for those key metrics, will be looking for some help. Of course, you are coming to offer help. One of the best ways to convince that senior leader is to demonstrate past successes. Work in your own backyard first to make your key linkages and discover your key causal drivers of outcomes in your own department. We found and identified specific invisible levers that existed in the work environment to reduce turnover, which then had quite a hefty cost savings for the organization. Take a look at those HR productivity numbers that you analyzed and helped you to discover the causal drivers. Now the other organizational leaders know that you know what you are talking about.

If you are trying this for the first time with a business partner, don't worry, a compelling story can be told without examples. The story, in fact, is a story you have told before. Most leaders buy-in to the notion that people are critical to success in any business-related initiative. The difference is that this time you are going to quantitatively demonstrate the impact of people-related metrics on the desired outcome. From there, you will be able to identify opportunities to improve the outcome and then prioritize them based on their impact. Finally, you will leverage your HR skills to develop and deploy initiatives that will causally impact the targeted outcome. The story is simple and decisions will be fact-based. Now you are speaking the language business leaders understand.

We recommend telling this story in a simple, straightforward manner. The story should go something like this:

1. An overview of the proposal: Empirically link employee data to critical business outcomes to determine opportunities and prioritize interventions.
2. An overview of the process: Gather relevant people and outcome data, create an integrated data file, conduct the empirical analysis, and then prioritize opportunities (refer to the Business Partner RoadMap™).
3. A proposed timeline: At a high level, outline the major steps and expected timing.
4. What you need to get started: Clearly state your need for his or her sponsorship and help identifying key stakeholders to involve.

You should have what you need to form the CFDT. The sponsorship of the leader will get you access to the appropriate stakeholders. Of course, the same sales pitch will need to be delivered to the other key stakeholders. The first meeting with key stakeholders needs to be structured and efficient. Prepare an agenda and identify the key outcomes of the meeting. The goal is to get everyone on board, as well as gather their input regarding the types of data that are available and how to go about gathering this data. By the end, you should be on your way to breaking down the silos that may exist. Of course, the silos will remain intact until you deliver results, but now you have the access you need to start the journey.

CHAPTER 12

Bringing Data Together to Find Solutions

We have provided examples and case studies demonstrating how to link various types of employee attitude and training data to sales, productivity, and turnover. Furthermore, in the Putting the Business Partner RoadMap™ to Work Case Study (Chapter 3), we provided an example of how to link all different kinds of employee data (e.g., competency ratings, training participation, dishonesty-related terminations, and employee-survey data) to a business outcome. In both cases, the prioritization of potential interventions is critical to focus resources, whether it is prioritizing interventions for multiple outcomes (i.e., sales, productivity, and turnover) or prioritizing numerous potential interventions for a single outcome (i.e., shrink). The purpose of this chapter is to provide an approach for prioritization and an easy way to "tell the story" that the linkage analysis reveals.

Prioritizing Interventions with Multiple Outcomes

It is safe to assume that sales, productivity, and turnover are the three most critical business outcomes for most organizations. In each individual case study, we conducted an analysis to identify the relationship between employee attitudes (along with some training data) and each identified outcome (e.g., sales). The problem is that by treating each outcome separately, we may identify three different lists of "invisible levers." That would mean a list of nine potential "invisible levers" across the three analyses. That number could be overwhelming for even the most sophisticated organizations. If we know anything, it is that being able to focus an organization on the critical few priorities is as important as anything in this process.

How do we overcome this potential barrier? The reality is that the analyses typically solve this issue for us. As discussed previously, all organizations are unique and each analysis will likely identify unique "levers" across organizations. However, it is also true that within an organization, two to three key "levers" typically emerge across outcomes. If you really think about this notion, it makes sense. The two or three facets of an organization's culture, that, if improved, would motivate an employee to be more productive, stay at an organization, or sell more of its products, are probably the same across outcomes, or at least overlap to some extent. Now, there will be nuances across outcomes, but, generally speaking, there will be some consistency in the themes. Figures 12.1, 12.2, and 12.3 represent examples of individual outcome models.

Figure 12.1 Sales Impact Model

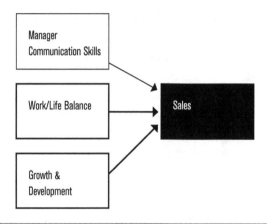

Figure 12.2 Productivity Impact Model

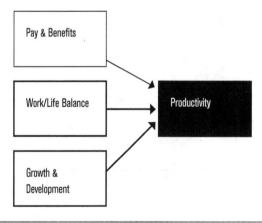

Figure 12.3 Turnover Impact Model

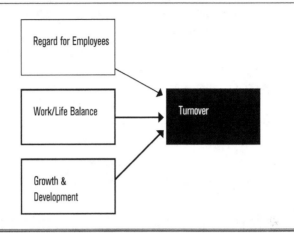

Summarizing the Findings

To increase sales, the organization should focus on improving manager communication skills, work/life balance, and growth and development. To increase productivity, the organization should focus on work/life balance, pay and benefits, and growth and development. To decrease turnover, the organization should focus on improving work/life balance, growth and development, and regard for employees. The integration across these individual models is pretty clear. Work/life balance, and growth and development, show up in all three models. Obviously, this should be the focus of the organization, given their business priorities. While the analysis isn't always this clean, we have never come upon an analysis without significant overlap of "invisible levers" of the various outcomes. But, of course, this does not mean it could not happen. In such a situation, we recommend prioritizing the interventions based on the strength of the relationship to the outcome, the implicit importance of the outcomes, and the ease/cost of building effective interventions. Essentially, pick the "lowest hanging fruit" with the strongest relationship with the most critical outcome (e.g., driving sales might be deemed to be more important than reducing turnover).

Two points are worth making regarding the integration of the different analyses. First of all, keeping the analysis focused at the survey-theme level is critical, as opposed to the individual-item level. Trying to initially integrate across analyses at the item level is difficult and really is not necessary, just yet. HR functions and business leaders think of "levers" in terms of these themes already, so it's not necessary to jump to the item level. Think of the integration process as if you were peeling back an onion. Start at the theme level and identify the major "levers." Then peel the onion back another layer and focus on the items. Prioritizing items within a theme can be done by understanding the items with the greatest empirical impact on the outcome measure and/or items with the lowest performance compared to relative benchmarks (e.g., norms from similar industries or similar-sized organizations). We recommend the combination of both approaches. It should be noted that the benchmarks are important to contextualize the data and effectively prioritize opportunities for improvement.

Again, this involves some advanced statistical knowledge (e.g., structural-equations modeling and multiple regression), but is actually pretty straightforward. Table 12.1 provides item-level information for the work/life balance, and growth and development themes for this example.

Based on our empirical analysis of the link between employee attitudes and the most critical outcomes, we identified that Growth and Development and Work/Life Balance were the two themes/domains with the greatest relationship to the desired outcomes. So, if we improve employee attitudes towards these items, we will improve sales, productivity, and turnover. In order to prioritize which survey items to work on, the item norms/benchmarks guide our prioritization. For the Growth and Development theme, items 3 and 5 are significantly lower than the industry benchmark. This suggests that for similar organizations, the organization being discussed performs significantly poorer on these two items. Thus, this analysis pinpoints the areas with the greatest room for improvement. It is apparent that employees do not (1) understand how to advance or (2) know what is required to achieve a promotion. Interventions should be focused in this area. Of course, further analysis can be done to pinpoint specific roles or functions where this problem exists. But, at a minimum, a systemic problem exists that needs to be addressed.

For the Work/Life Balance theme, a similar analysis reveals three items that are problematic (6, 7, and 10). These items also reveal a consistent "story." While the organization appears to support Work/Life Balance programs in general, managers are having difficulty executing the programs. Employees are not able to take time off or use "floating" days when the need arises. Again, systemic interventions should be developed to address these opportunities for improvement.

Prioritizing Interventions with a Single Outcome

Let us now consider instances where we are attempting to prioritize interventions based on the linkage analysis of multiple people data sources and a single outcome variable, like in the Putting the Business Partner RoadMap™ to Work Case Study

Table 12.1 Survey Items for Work/Life Balance and Growth & Development

Item	Mean Score (5-point scale)	Difference from Benchmark
Growth and Development		
1. My "career talk" with my immediate supervisor or manager during the last year provided me with useful feedback.	4.11	0.02
2. I am able to discuss career opportunities at XYZ with my manager.	3.97	-0.03
3. I know what I need to do in order to be considered for advancement.	3.29	-0.24
4. I have received the training needed to do my job effectively.	4.22	0.11
5. I understand the responsibilities and skills that are necessary to be considered for advancement.	3.31	-0.19
Work/Life Balance		
6. I am able to take time off when I need it (i.e., planned vacation, etc).	3.32	-0.29
7. In general, my immediate manager helps employees balance work and personal responsibilities.	3.29	-0.15
8. The work environment at XYZ supports a balance between work and personal life.	3.79	0.02
9. Senior leaders value and support work/life balance initiatives.	4.10	0.22
10. I am able to take time off when unexpected personal needs arise.	3.22	0.42

Case Study presented earlier. In this instance, the primary means of prioritization is the empirical relationship to the outcome measure. In other words, pick the interventions with the greatest impact on the desired outcome. The Putting the Business Partner RoadMap™ to Work Case Study outlines this process in great detail, so we won't rehash all of it again. Suffice it to say that the prioritization process is much simpler as the magnitude of the relationships to the outcome will clearly provide a means of prioritization. However, the "low hanging fruit" principle still applies here as well. Much like the process of building any business case, a small investment with moderate returns may still be preferred over a large investment with moderate to larger returns. For example, in the Putting the Business Partner RoadMap™ to Work Case Study, we found completion of the mandatory ethics course was moderately related to shrink. In this example, while participation was mandatory, the organization was far from achieving full compliance. It was determined that, with a relatively small investment of resources, the organization could significantly increase employee compliance with the training requirement. One last point: Benchmark data can also be used in a single-outcome instance. Again, the benchmarks will help contextualize the data and identify opportunities for improvement.

CHAPTER 13

Creating Metrics
That Drive Results

Merely finding key causal drivers and creating/implementing initiatives around them is not the end-all, be-all of Human Resources. We must also be able to hold ourselves accountable for implementing solid programs and initiatives around those key causal drivers. Creating sound metrics around what we are doing will solidify that accountability and give HR leaders yet another opportunity to reach the status of trusted advisor and to have a respected voice in the boardroom.

Creating metrics is as much about the numbers and the math as it is about the buy-in and communication of the metrics. This book is all about the crucial first step of determining what to set the metric around. We have covered this extensively.

The second step is to ensure that the measurement process behind the metrics make sense to the organization. For example, if a metric is set around employee attitudes and your organization's balanced scorecard is published twice per month, it may not make complete sense to survey employees constantly just so that a new number is available every two weeks. The same goes for competency ratings. It would be nearly impossible to have a fresh round of competency ratings, even for a monthly balanced scorecard. So, setting realistic expectations for senior leaders around how often the numbers will be updated on the balanced scorecard will help you to avoid problems later. These potential problems really center about leaders, from the front line to the senior-executive level, who will want to see their numbers change (improve) every time the balanced scorecard is published. Who wants to be saddled with a low employee-opinion survey score for their branch when it is only conducted annually? Be careful of the drumbeat for an ongoing, year-round survey or, worse, eliminating the survey score from the balanced scorecard altogether.

Next, you want to truly over-communicate any new metrics, or adjustments to current metrics. And always be wary of changing goals because many individuals' performance ratings and bonuses are at stake. The good news about the Business Partner RoadMap™ is that you now have a sound rationale for not only changing the metrics, but also demonstrating how and why the metrics are related to business outcomes. Communicating the metrics will require a solid "road-show" effort on your part. In our experience, after showing the impact of the metrics on business outcomes that leaders care about, the metrics communication experience will improve dramatically. An essential piece to the road-show is to also communicate what you, in Human Resources, will be doing to support leaders in reaching their goals on these metrics. Do not forget the front-line manager's perspective of what they truly care about. You now will have metrics that do not exist in a vacuum, but that actually mean something to those metrics that front-line managers need to achieve. It is imperative to also show the organization what you will be implementing in terms of training, initiatives, communications, etc., to get them to those metric goals.

Example of Metrics for Key Drivers

In the first case study, at the large retail organization that was focused on product shrink, the company discovered that the following key drivers of that business outcome were:

1. Achieving Outstanding Results Competency.
2. Reducing Dishonesty Terminations.
3. Participating in the Sales/Product-Shrink Training Course.
4. Participating in the Ethics Training Course.
5. Employee Attitudes about Customer Focus, Job-Person Match, and Policies.

For the first key driver, the metric that was recommended was to increase the percentage of managers that were rated a 4 or 5 on that competency from 10 percent currently to 25 percent. The organization set this metric with the knowledge that this managerial competency is directly linked to improved product shrink. The rationale behind the increase was that, based on the initiatives, training, and coaching to be implemented, managers' performance would increase and that would be reflected in their competency ratings on their annual performance reviews. You may be thinking that these scores can be easily manipulated by the senior manager (by rating his or her managers higher). This is always a risk, but the check-and-balance is in place to compare the managers' actual numbers to the previous year to see if they truly have "achieved outstanding results." This severely reduces the temptation to inflate ratings, if those managers being rated have not achieved outstanding results.

The second key driver of product shrink was "Reducing Dishonesty Terminations." Annually, the organization currently was experiencing 10 percent of their terminations due to dishonesty. The metric for the organization was set to reach five percent of terminations due to dishonesty for the year. We wish that there was an exact science around the setting of goals for metrics. This goal was set to cut in half the number of dishonesty terminations. The buy-in was achieved by a full review of the new selection instruments that were being put in place (e.g., integrity tests and ethics courses). The organization also wanted to set an aggressive goal for this, as it represented a direct loss of goods and hit store profitability instantly. The check-and-balance here is the constant monitoring of the store's product-shrink numbers, which do reflect dishonesty (i.e. theft) in the workplace. Human Resources is getting buy-in not only for the new metric, but also for the new selection instruments, because they can now demonstrate the connection between the two and they have given front-line managers an effective upstream weapon to battle dishonesty in their stores via a more effective hiring process.

The third key driver of product shrink was shown to be the percentage of all employees, at the store level, who had completed the organization's ethics training course in the past year. Currently, the organization had a completion rate of just 68 percent (as you recall, this was a "mandatory" course). Not surprisingly, the metric was set to reach a 100 percent completion rate for the year, and every year after that. More importantly, all of the organization's leaders were on board with this, and not because of their embarrassment at only hitting 68 percent completion on a course that everyone should take. What has changed is that they no longer look at the ethics training course as a box to check as they are getting an employee started on their first few days of work. The new attitude is that, yes, they need to get these courses completed, and that everyone should re-take the course annually. Managers now co-lead many of the sessions to drive home key points — and drive down their product-shrink numbers.

The final key drivers of product shrink came from employee attitudes, specifically: Customer Focus, Job-Person Match, and Policies. So, rather than setting a metric that focuses on overall employee satisfaction or engagement — which is a generic measure of employee attitudes — the metrics were set around a strong, significant improvement in these three key areas of the work environment. The metrics were set to reach a statistically significant improvement on all of the items that make up these three areas of employee attitudes.

To be clear, statistical significance is heavily weighted by the sample size (i.e., the number of employees that complete the survey). So please be careful when setting goals that are "statistically" significant. If your organization has many thousands of employees, then statistical significance may mean an extremely small increase. This may not sit well with senior leaders to see only a 0.01 increase on an item being referred to as significant. This is why getting early buy-in from various stakeholders is important. We also mentioned that there is not an exact science around goal-setting. This is one of those times where setting a goal with "practical" significance is appropriate, because the science in this case is working at odds with organizational goals.

We need to account for the possibility that employee-opinion survey scores can be manipulated by managers, via bribes, threats, etc. This is a rare occurrence but it is something that needs to be discussed. Guaranteeing anonymity on the survey for all employees, and gaining manager buy-in as to why the initiatives behind these metrics have been shown to be effective in helping them reach their goals, are the two most important components to eradicate "gaming" the system. Yes, it is still possible that managers will "teach the test" or constantly reinforce to employees that it is important for them to score certain items very highly. We understand that there are risks involved. However, the measurements and tracking that you put in place for your HR metrics will provide the checks-and-balances needed to discover any disconnects between what managers are doing and the results that they are getting on, for example, the Customer Focus items on the employee survey.

The HR Balanced Scorecard

The organization's overall balanced scorecard will contain the metrics discussed above under the banner of "People." This is a big win for the HR function, but, as we mentioned, the checks-and-balances for these metrics, as well as the need to hold ourselves accountable to goals, is also critical. We do realize that any metric can be "gamed," so it is extremely important to have a solid base of interventions that will actually drive the metric. These interventions, of course, can be measured with a host of HR-specific metrics as well.

Your HR balanced scorecard needs to contain metrics that hold your HR leaders accountable for the effective implementation of the initiatives that you have discovered drive your business outcomes. There is a striking difference between what has typically been done in the past and what is done today. In the past, you may have had "survey participation rate" and "days-to-fill a job" as key metrics. These are important, but are they connected in any way to improving the organization? Did we have any analytics behind them to "sell" them to front-line managers? In the first case study, Human Resources now tracks itself on ethics course completion, and has added a quick test at the end to measure how well the course was conducted. Second, with the new selection instrument being introduced throughout the organization, HR leaders held themselves accountable for getting all front-line managers trained on the new instruments by a specific date and tracked the use of the instruments at each store. Most importantly, Human Resources was also held accountable to the outcome (not just the activities) of the new selection instruments — the organization's metric on "reducing dishonesty terminations."

For the "Achieving Outstanding Results" competency, HR leaders were held accountable for (1) the completion of the product-shrink assessment program that discovered key skills and behaviors of top- and bottom-performing product-shrink managers and (2) the shrink partnership program that involved pairing up high and low performers on product shrink. The metrics for the HR leaders centered around getting the assessment completed and the ongoing facilitation of the shrink partnership program. As with the dishonesty terminations metric, Human Resources was also held accountable for the outcomes of its activities — increasing the overall level of managers receiving scores of a 4 or 5 on the "Achieving Outstanding Results" competency. Just to beat a dead horse, the entire organization was on board with this particular metric because the causal linkage between the competency and the critical business outcome (i.e., product shrink) had been clearly articulated and thoroughly communicated to them.

This is really where the inherent value of using analytics-based metrics in your organization — the buy-in from leaders/managers and the ability to show an impact — really pays off. When you think about the "classic" HR metrics, such as time-to-fill, you might want to take a step back and use the analytics approach in the Business Partner RoadMap™ to determine the impact of decreasing your time-to-fill metric (see Table 13.1). Are groups that make faster hiring decisions experiencing lower turnover? Have you made the causal connection between those "classic" HR metrics and a relevant business outcome? As we will discuss at length in the next chapter, managers will focus on what is being measured on the balanced scorecard. By incorporating analytics-based metrics, you will have created a set of metrics that go from being a "to-do" list for front-line managers to being a "must-do for success" list.

Table 13.1. Traditional vs. Analytics-based HR Metrics

Traditional HR Metric	Analytics-Based Metric
Overall Turnover	Dishonesty Terminations
Overall Satisfaction/Engagement	Customer Focus/Job Match
Overall Training Completion	Ethics Course Completion
Overall Performance Appraisal Completion	"Achieve Extraordinary Results Competency Rating Improvement"

CHAPTER 14

The Front-Line Manager's View

It is an understatement to say that front-line managers have too much on their plates. Their days are filled with requests from customers, employees, and, of course, other functions within the organization requesting all types of data/reports and other activities that soak up their precious time. After all that work from the other internal functions is completed, hopefully they can get back to their actual job of delivering service and making money for the company.

Front-line managers need all the help they can get, not because they aren't capable, but because of the ongoing tug-of-war with their time. It should not be a surprise that many front-line managers, no matter how enlightened, don't exactly look at the HR function as a place to find balanced-scorecard salvation. Without any data to prove that their initiatives are actually linked to important business metrics, a manager's HR involvement will continue to be viewed as time not-so-well spent.

In their opinion, Human Resources, for the most part, just adds work to their plates without any connection to any real tangible benefits. The typical expectation of Human Resources by front-line managers is for Human Resources to help front-line managers find people to hire, raise their employee-opinion survey scores, and investigate employee concerns.

Principle 3: Employee engagement in itself is *not* a business outcome.

The Importance of Front-Line Managers

Organizational leaders can make large capital investments, sweeping changes in company policy, and major strategic moves, but that can ultimately mean little if they cannot get their entire management team on board. Front-line managers not only manage employees on a day-to-day basis but, according to recent research,[1] also must be a "liaison" between senior management and front-line employees. In order to win the hearts and minds of these managers, every organizational change, large or small, needs to address the almighty "what's-in-it-for-me" premise. Your front-line managers are held accountable for, and are obsessed with, a specific set of measures. Typically, on the balanced scorecard, raises, bonuses, and career progression are normally tied directly to performance. It makes sense, then, that front-line managers would reach out to any function in the organization for help if it meant gaining an edge in achieving balanced-scorecard glory. Now, think of the front-line managers in your organization. Are they calling their local HR representatives to beg them to get their people signed up for the latest training on management 101 or the workshop on how to make the most of their employee-survey data? Probably not. HR managers are likely spending their days "encouraging" front-line managers to get excited about the training. As mentioned above, front-line managers do not look to Human Resources to help them reach their balanced-scorecard goals. This is not just the fault of Human Resources. Front-line managers should look to Human Resources to help them with their balanced-scorecard quest, but HR needs to give those managers a reason to seek out their services.

Principle 10: Perceptions alone do not show up on the P&L statement.

Beyond the Balanced Scorecard

We wish that we could say that your organization's balanced-scorecard metrics are the only numbers to which your front-line managers are held accountable. Remember, every other function in the organization has an initiative that is extremely important, and that ultimately falls on the front-line managers' shoulders. Just to name a few:

- 401(k) Enrollment
- Workers' Compensation Reduction
- Accident Reduction
- Employee Survey Participation
- Finance Reports
- New Computer Technology Training Participation
- Part-time Turnover

Just to reiterate, this is in addition to customer calls, employee complaints, and accomplishing the laundry list of tasks that need to be completed as part of that manager's day job. They need to know what drives these metrics to help get them accomplished, so they can be successful. Your organization has the data available to reveal these invisible levers, which will make all of your front-line managers successful, and ultimately, your entire organization successful. But there are obstacles.

The HR Obstacle

From the front-line manager view, Human Resources creates more work (e.g., more paperwork/busy work — such as getting people to fill out the opinion survey), but does Human Resources ever really help front-line managers make more money? The answer is yes. The problem is that Human Resources doesn't know how to uncover this impact or how to take credit for it.

Phil Rosenzweig has made the assertion that "happy" employees don't cause high performance in organizations, but rather that high organizational performance causes employees to be happy.[2] Rosenzweig goes on to say that HR leaders, in order to get a seat at the table, should focus on the skill capabilities that drive performance. Fair enough. But where is the data that proves skill capabilities are causally related to any relevant business outcomes? Front-line managers often loathe sending people off-site to attend training (or even attend themselves), when they are pessimistic as to how that training will help them achieve their operational metrics. These managers do not believe that their people will come back "fixed" and suddenly be more productive than they were before attending the training.

For decades, Human Resources has traded on the currency (i.e., assumption) that happy employees lead to better performance. We aren't saying that this premise has no merit, but let's be sure that the evidence is strong, compelling, and statistically sound. You will be able to do this in your organization with our process.

HR as Front-line Partner

For Human Resources to truly become an asset in the relentless pursuit of business-outcome metrics, they must begin a serious quest to find out what drives those metrics, and create programs and initiatives to drive them. In our experience, organizations will have at least 20 metrics on their balanced scorecard, and at least another five to seven key strategic initiatives that carry their own metrics; in all, at least 25 opportunities to begin linking key drivers to critical business outcomes that senior and front-line managers truly care about. Front-line managers will want to know the invisible levers that they can pull to reach their goals on these 25 metrics. As mentioned in Chapter 2, this again shows why generic information gathered from completely different organizations and compiled into a short list of "magic bullets" is not effective for your organization to be successful. You have metrics and strategic initiatives that are completely unique to your organization. Attempting to train your front-line managers on generic skills from some business book or a best practices workshop is like firing a shotgun at a bull's eye — sure you may get a few quality hits, but most will fall woefully off-target.

Only, in this case, you can count the misses in dollars, time, and credibility that you wasted by being off-target.

Instead of going on-site to one of your branches armed with the latest consultant-speak program on how to raise employee happiness, your front-line manager at that branch would love to see the data that shows the direct business impact your current initiative has. This moves you from an "us-vs.–them" relationship to a relationship where the front-line manager wants to invest his or her time in your program because the returns will be there on the other side.

CHAPTER 15

Invisible Levers for External Business Challenges

Today's business environment is constantly changing, and different challenges are always arising that leaders must face and overcome. When it comes to the workforce, there are specific challenges that Human Resources needs to master in order to have a meaningful impact.

Managing a Global Workforce

In managing a global workforce, we know that individuals from different cultures have varied expectations and motivations when it comes to their day-to-day employment. There are plenty of books and articles that have reported and continue to report on this issue.[1] Rather than rely on what different cultural expectations and motivations are *assumed* to be, we suggest you use your data and apply our process to discover the true invisible levers that impact your bottom lines outside the United States. The same structure applies outside of the United States, in that you will need to determine what strategic outcomes are critical for that international portion of the business. It is important not to assume that the strategic outcomes in the United States are equivalent to the strategic outcomes in international operations as, many times, they are (recently) a growth engine for a U.S.-based organization. Our point is that the key-stakeholder interviews are just as important when examining international invisible levers as they are when examining domestic invisible levers. You will need to follow the same process (the Business Partner RoadMap™), the key difference being that you will just use the people data and business outcomes in the particular country that you are examining. One drawback is the need to have enough data to conduct a meaningful analysis. This is where a statistician will be useful — they will let you know the sample size that you will need in order to move forward.

The Multi-Generational and Aging Workforce

We know that the topic of Generation X (born between 1964 and 1980) and Generation Y (born after 1980), the Baby Boomers (born between 1946 and

1963), and the Silent Generation (born between 1925 and 1945) has gotten enough press that business leaders are well aware of these groups and their different wants, needs, and motivations. Additionally, the workforce is aging. According to Susan Meisinger, former president and CEO of the Society for Human Resource Management, "the federal workforce is older, five years or so on average … we're starting to see the bigger companies taking steps to keep older people."[2] Unfortunately, as with all of the topics we have covered thus far, broad and sweeping generalizations have been made about each generational cohort based just on a few studies (sound familiar?). It is dangerous to apply conclusions that have been drawn by researchers across numerous types of organizations, to your organization. Not all Generation Y employees are dying to work from home and only care about themselves, and not all Baby Boomers are looking to retire on their 65th birthday, nor are they all great "company men" who would not ever think of switching jobs. What is important is that you gather/capture the people data and bottom-line data to determine the invisible levers that cause these different generations to deliver the desired results. Many times, an employee-opinion survey will allow you to capture these generational characteristics that exist amongst employees in your organization.

We recently worked with a large technology company that was struggling with losing people across the generational spectrum to competitors. They told us point-blank that they "read up" on the different generations and applied creative solutions to deal with what they thought were the proven reasons why these generational cohorts were turning over. After applying our process in this organization, we found that the different generations were not leaving because of what the popular press/broad research was saying. Thankfully, this organization let their own data do the talking and created initiatives that were relevant to their own employees, not to watered-down generational similarities (averages). Turnover has fallen by 28 percent in this particular organization, with an ROI of 58 percent.

The Growing Part-time Workforce

The part-time workforce is growing quickly, and as they become more impactful on the bottom line, it becomes more critical to discover the invisible levers that can be pulled to maximize their impact.[3] This is another topic that is gaining momentum in the popular press and will likely lead to many generalizations about this sector of the workforce. It will also lead to new products for consulting firms to try to sell to you that have been "proven" to work. Thankfully, you know better because you hired your part-timers, they have become a part of your organization's culture, and have either bought into it or exited the organization. But this is definitely a distinct set of employees who can vary from college students to retirees. You do have the data necessary to pinpoint the invisible levers that you can pull to impact this critical group. The goals for this group can be different based on the stakeholder interviews. Many of the organizations that we work with focus on minimizing turnover and pinpointing the types of benefits that will attract strong part-timers to them. In one particular organization, we were told by senior leadership that "shift flexibility" was the reason many part-timers joined, and why they stayed with them. Not surprisingly, this was based on history and assumptions, and not based on any data.

Using our process, we found shift flexibility did play a role in retention, but, using their employee-opinion data and demographic data, the key invisible levers were alignment with mission/values, communication from local management, and participating in programs and initiatives normally reserved specifically for full-timers. We also dug deeper to find alignment with mission/values was the invisible lever that drove part-timers to not only stay with the organization, but also to stay on to become full-timers. When we presented this information to leadership, they bought in immediately, once they realized that part-timers have a lot of flexibility to move to any organization they want — the perception is there are plenty of part-time jobs to be had, and that is likely true. Thus, part-timers really do not want to be treated like part-time "help" by their managers simply because they can leave easily. In addition, they wanted to believe the organization lived up to its mission and values statement because that was a key invisible lever that made them consider this particular organization as a place they would want to work full-time. Finally, the data revealed a desire, on the side of the part-timers, to participate in full-time initiatives, such as sales contests. This also shone light on the fact that the part-timers being hired at this organization were not only there because they wanted a part-time job, they were there because they wanted (at least eventually) a full-time job. Management is now treating these individuals as full-time employees who happen to work part-time.

After applying the Business Partner RoadMap™ in the organization we just described, and building initiatives around the proven invisible levers, turnover dropped 32 percent in the first eight months, and part-time to full-time transitions are up 61 percent.

Transforming Human Resources

The Business Partner RoadMap™ is effective in allowing HR leaders to determine the invisible levers that drive business outcomes. This process has transformed how the HR function delivers value to organizations. The long-term goal, however, should be that Human Resources is a major player in the overall direction of the organization. To that end, this final section will show how you can use the RoadMap to drive the overall strategy of Human Resources, and how to gain the coveted seat at the table and achieve "trusted advisor" status in the eyes of your customers.

CHAPTER 16

Setting HR Strategy

Many HR strategy and budgeting meetings can be effective at plotting a course for the coming year. Organizations spend numerous days discussing talent management, succession planning, benefits, compensation, 401(k) plans, training plans, etc. However, many times this meeting can turn into a discussion that focuses entirely on how to cut costs from the HR budget. Unfortunately, if Human Resources is still viewed as a cost-only function, this may be the only topic that is discussed at these meetings. Using the Business Partner RoadMap™ to unveil the invisible levers that can be pulled to impact business outcomes in your organization will allow you to move from a purely cost-based HR strategy meeting to setting a strategy that focuses on investments that are ROI- and analytics-based.

The strategy process is always complicated, and it is made more so for Human Resources if the function is not aligned with the strategies of the other functions within the organization. The stakeholder interviews that we urge HR leaders to conduct will provide a solid first step in aligning the strategy process with the rest of the business. After conducting all of the analyses that show where the strongest and most effective investments in people should be made, the strategy meetings can become focused on "how much is Human Resources going to add to the financial health of this organization?" vs. "how much can we cut out this year?" Keep in mind, in serious economic situations, the cost cuts will need to be made, but changing the attitude of the organization as a whole towards Human Resources will make the outcomes of the strategy and budget meetings more business-impact focused, vs. being purely cost-focused.

Principle 1: Organizations already spend significant amounts of money on their people ... they just don't spend it on the right things.

Much of this book has focused on a one-off approach using the Business Partner RoadMap™. While the Roadmap can be applied in many settings, there is also a recommended approach for organizations that aligns with their strategic-planning process. Most organizations conduct an annual strategy-planning and financial-planning process, starting a quarter or so prior to the beginning of the next fiscal year. We recommend that the Business Partner RoadMap™ process to identify invisible levers be performed during this planning process. The timing on conducting the analyses should be three to four months before the beginning of your fiscal year. This timeline will give your organization enough time to complete all of the steps in the Business Partner RoadMap™ and make key decisions on prioritizing what to work on. From a people perspective, the results of the Business Partner RoadMap™will inform strategy, budgeting, and metric setting, so it makes sense for an organization to incorporate the RoadMap process into their existing, annual strategic-planning process. This ensures that people-related initiatives are aligned with key strategic priorities, are appropriately funded, and are associated with an expected ROI. When this occurs, the role of HR is clearly linked to the strategic priorities of the organization. After all, that is the ultimate goal of our approach. Figure 16.1 shows how the RoadMap is aligned with the typical organizational planning timeline.

Figure 16.1 Typical Organizational Planning Cycle

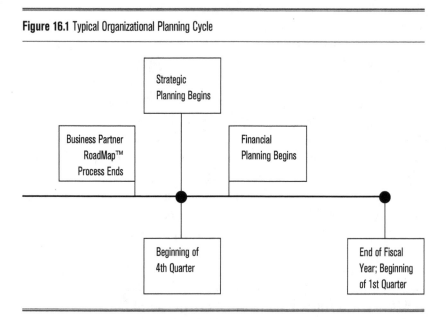

CHAPTER 17

HR's "Seat at the Table"

There are numerous conferences, roundtables, and presentations every year that are geared toward HR professionals, as well as our quest to get a "seat at the table" with business leaders. The ironic twist: When it is time for Human Resources to prove its worth and show actual value, we often fall short of that goal. We fall short in empirically connecting what we do in Human Resources (which is very important) to any crucial business outcomes. The idea of showing outcomes in the form of HR efficiencies or broad correlations between people data and bottom-line metrics such as company profitability is not what is needed to get a seat at the table. As HR partners, we all want business leaders to "agree" that what we do is important, and most organizational leaders do agree that Human Resources is important — but they do so without solid quantitative proof. Simple "agreement," without facts, likely will not translate into a meaningful seat at the table.

We also cannot overlook the fact that by having a seat at the table, it subsequently means having a "hot" seat at the table. That seat comes with a high level of accountability for results — business results. If we want a seat at the table, we need to understand the consequences of having that seat. Showing impact with analysis, like every other senior executive, will earn that HR leader a seat and also earn him or her a hefty amount of accountability to improve the top and bottom lines of the organization. The point is not to create reservations about getting what we all want. Rather, the point is to prepare us for the increased accountability that comes with a greater role in our organizations. The goal of this book is to provide a framework and pragmatic approach to earning this proverbial "seat at the table."

Principle 8: Once a connection/linkage is made with the data, accountability is unavoidable (and that's a good thing).

"Why We Hate HR" — What Can We Learn?

The cover article in the August 2005 issue of *Fast Company* was "Why We Hate HR." It was not done tongue-in-cheek. The author of the article, Keith Hammonds, was fed up with the HR function and did not hold back in his rhetoric. According to Hammonds:

> After close to 20 years of hopeful rhetoric about becoming "strategic partners" with a "seat at the table" where the business decisions that matter are made, most human-resources professionals aren't nearly there. They have no seat, and the table is locked inside a conference room to which they have no key. HR people are, for most practical purposes, neither strategic nor leaders. ... The human-resources trade long ago proved itself, at best, a necessary evil — and at worst, a dark bureaucratic force that blindly enforces nonsensical rules, resists creativity, and impedes constructive change. HR is the corporate function with the greatest potential — the key driver, in theory, of business performance — and also the one that most consistently under-delivers.[1]

It has been a few years since that article was published. Have things changed? In a September 2007 article from *Workforce Management*, only 17 percent of HR leaders said that one of their top challenges was "measuring the contribution of human capital."[2] So how do we move beyond this bad reputation?

Making These Articles and Surveys a Thing of the Past

We are just as frustrated as you are by all of these surveys, charts, and articles that talk about Human Resources being disconnected from the bottom line of the organization. Accenture's *High-Performance Workforce Study* from 2006 noted that only 12 percent of senior executives rated their Human Resources and Training functions as highly effective at aligning workforce skills to business priorities.[3] We know there are many more of these studies out there; we got tired of looking for them, and we got tired of reading their depressing results. This is one of many key reasons why we wrote this book — because we want to see studies that talk about how 100 percent of senior executives cannot have a meeting about anything without input from Human Resources.

HR Fads

Another disturbing issue with Human Resources is the constant array of concepts and catchphrases that bloom into vogue every few years. "Employee engagement" was one of the recent fads, while "quality circles" and "leaderless teams" have also come and gone. There are countless others that we could mention, but let's not pile on. The point here is that having constant fads, and new concepts regarding how to lead organizations, is a credibility killer. What makes the situation worse is that most of these fads and new concepts are coined and driven by consultants — not customers — and they always seem to be based on intuition and neatly contrived models and not on thorough data collected and analyzed in your organization. It is amazing how frequently consultants can come up with nice-sounding concepts using clever acronyms that suddenly become useful in all industries worldwide, in both the public and private sectors, which are based upon limited proof and suspect data. This is especially true when your business function has a reputation for having a constant stream of fads and new concepts. In comparison, the procurement function rarely has a new fad that dictates how they conduct their work, nor does the finance organization. If the operations function wants to try something new, they will pilot-test the heck out of it to see if it actually works before investing in it. Now, when operations or other functions actually do change the way they work, they must come up with exact costs of the investment and a defined ROI. Is Human Resources always held to that standard? No! A new book comes out that has a cute acronym and interesting title and suddenly that training program must be implemented company-wide as soon as possible. If we sound excited, it is because we are. Our approach presented here shows you how to set a data-driven HR strategy (certainly not a fad).

So, as a profession, let's not be susceptible to these fads. To do this, we need to make decisions based on facts and data that demonstrate an empirical link between our initiatives and meaningful business outcomes. The excuse that what we do is not quantifiable is bogus. Anything can be measured, and we can empirically link any measurement (e.g., participation in training) to another measurement (e.g., financial metrics). By doing this, we can demonstrate the impact of what we do on the bottom line.

HR Is Aware of the Situation

HR professionals are well aware of the challenges that organizations face. The 2008 SHRM Workplace Forecast revealed the "Key Priorities for HR Professionals as They Prepare for the Future."[4] They are, in order of importance:
1. Improving Leadership Development
2. Managing Talent
3. Delivering on Recruiting and Staffing
4. Managing Change and Cultural Transformation

5.   Managing Demographics — Aging Workforce
6.   Enhancing Employee Commitment
7.   Transforming Human Resources into a Strategic Partner
8.   Managing Work/Life Balance
9.   Improving Performance Management and Rewards
10. Managing Diversity

It is great to see that all of these issues are on the minds of HR professionals, because they are all critical. More importantly (this is where we all need to challenge ourselves), every one of these issues have distinct causes and effects. To be a strategic partner in your organization, it is imperative to discover the invisible levers that are causing these issues, as well as the financial impact that they have on your organization. This book is offering you the tools to take on this challenge and to be successful in your goal of becoming a strategic business partner.

CHAPTER 18

Trusted Advisor Status

Most of us have heard HR professionals talking about becoming "trusted advisors" to the business leaders they support. So what does that mean? We believe that the status of trusted advisor has been achieved when an HR professional is seen as more than an HR subject-matter expert. This means your business partner asks for your input on topics outside of hiring, firing, training, etc. Ultimately, your input is valued on business-related issues, not just people-related issues. We will break this down shortly so it does not seem overwhelming. Our goal is to lay out a step-by-step approach for becoming a trusted advisor. The authors of *The Trusted Advisor* detailed the skills needed to become a trusted advisor to clients (as consultants).[1] This was great information (and, of course, still is). Table 18.1 shows the benefits that come from being trusted by clients.

Table 18.1. Benefits of Being a Trusted Advisor

The more clients trust you, the more they will:

1. Reach for your advice.
2. Be inclined to accept and act on your recommendations.
3. Bring you in on more advanced, complex, and strategic issues.
4. Treat you as you wish to be treated.
5. Respect you.
6. Share more information that helps you to help them, and improves the quality of the service you provide.
7. Pay your bills without question.
8. Refer you to their friends and business acquaintances.
9. Lower the level of stress in your interactions.
10. Give you the benefit of the doubt.
11. Forgive you when you make a mistake.
12. Protect you when you need it.
13. Warn you of dangers that you might avoid.
14. Be comfortable and allow you to be comfortable.
15. Involve you early on when their issues begin to form, rather than later in the process (or maybe even call you first).
16. Trust your instincts and judgments (including those about other people such as your colleagues and theirs).

Before we describe how to become a trusted HR advisor, let's first discuss who is *not* a trusted HR advisor. Throughout our years as internal and external consultants, as well as in our roles as line-of-business leaders, we have worked with many types of HR partners. Some of these HR partners have been highly effective at achieving a "trusted advisor" status; others have not. We have tried to generalize a bit regarding the profiles of these not-so-effective HR partners. Stick with us on this and please don't take offense. The purpose is not to trivialize our HR counterparts, but rather to learn from their strengths and their weaknesses. In our experiences, we have identified four distinct types of ineffective HR partners.

The Execution Expert

We believe that many relatively successful HR partners fit into this profile. These are the HR professionals who have become masters at executing HR-related tasks (e.g., hiring, firing, HR process implementation, managing personnel expense, implementing layoffs). We all know how important executing tasks and processes are to Human Resources and, for that matter, nearly all business roles. Often, this type of HR professional is highly rated in execution-oriented roles. Obviously, they get a lot done, and do it well. They are often labeled as "task masters" and are highly conscientious. These are all good things. On the negative side, often this type of HR partner gets labeled as transactional and is seen as a paper or process pusher. Line-of-business partners often do not see the value of the tasks they are completing and complain about completing forms or executing processes that take them away from "real" work. Furthermore, this type of partner usually hits a ceiling in their career as they struggle to grow into more strategic, advisor-oriented roles. These roles are typically more senior in nature. Furthermore, the ones that do move into senior roles become order-takers from their line-of-business partners and struggle to become a true advisor to their clients. Unfortunately, the "Execution Expert" keeps his or her head down the entire time and does not look at the big picture or connect those numerous tasks to any business outcomes.

The Executive Coach

Again, we have encountered several HR partners who would fit into this type and who have been extremely successful in their HR careers. This particular type of partner is great at establishing credibility with line-of-business partners. They quickly move into a coach or advisor role. They are skilled at engaging their clients and offering sound advice related to people issues. The worst examples of this type can sometimes be referred to as "empty suits." When this label is used, what it really means is that the person talks a good game and sounds extremely credible. However, they usually either struggle with execution and producing results or they lack true HR expertise. Sometimes, this type of HR partner actually rises quickly in the ranks and may even be seen as a "high potential" HR associate early in their career. However, this same "high potential" employee can fall from grace just as quickly. This usually results from giving bad advice (e.g., poor hiring decisions, ineffective organizational change), a lack of producing HR-related results (e.g., low employee engagement, significant turnover), or simply through an inability to execute effectively.

The Risk Manager

This type of HR partner typically receives the most complaints from front-line managers. This occurs when an HR partner consistently tells a manager what they cannot do. It is true that a significant role of an HR professional is to protect an organization from litigation and ensure adherence to organizational values/ethics. However, it becomes a problem for some HR partners when this role becomes their primary function. Furthermore, some HR partners say "no" often and subsequently provide few solutions. From the line-of-business' view, HR is creating a barrier to the performance of the business. The most common example occurs when a manager wants to fire a poor performer, especially if the targeted poor performer is a member of a protected demographic. We are not suggesting that the HR partner's advice is not valid; rather, we are suggesting that it can create a poor perception from the manager's perspective. This perception only becomes a problem when an HR partner continuously says "no" and offers little value beyond risk management. We believe that every time an HR partner creates a barrier to performance, he or she needs to create at least two enhancements to performance. Similar to the Execution Expert, the Risk Manager can be successful in lower-level HR roles, but often has difficulty advancing to more senior-level positions. The cause is simple. The HR professional may not be viewed by operations managers as a business partner and is primarily responsible for creating barriers to performance.

The Subject-Matter Expert

This type of HR partner is often an HR specialist learning to be an HR generalist, or a generalist who relies too strongly on his or her area of expertise. It is true that we all have different areas of expertise, often depending upon our educational background and our previous job experience. Furthermore, we are not suggesting that specializing in one particular HR area (e.g., leadership development, compensation, staffing) is not important. In fact, specialists are required within successful HR functions to bring depth and expertise to the organization. Rather, we are referring to the instances where our lack of breadth in all HR areas creates a barrier to becoming a trusted HR advisor. The primary impediment to achieving the status of trusted advisor is an over-reliance on too-specific knowledge and skills. For example, an HR partner with significant depth in leadership development will sometimes overuse this skill, such that nearly all problems or interventions will involve the development of leaders. The issue for the business is that they receive very limited support that may not adequately address issues or achieve the desired results. Job rotations that become part of the career path to senior HR jobs would certainly help to alleviate this particular issue.

Using the Profiles to Your Advantage

So we have spent a lot of time describing what a trusted HR advisor is not. We did this because these profiles also contain attributes of what a trusted advisor should be. By taking the best of these profiles and balancing their strengths, the status of trusted advisor can be achieved. Let's consider a balanced approach that is inclusive of all four attributes:

1. Execution of HR processes.
2. Advising and coaching business leaders.
3. Managing organizational risk.
4. Providing HR subject-matter expertise.

When an HR partner effectively balances these four primary roles and aligns those activities with the overall business' strategy, then and only then will the status of trusted advisor be achieved. This sounds simple, but there is a bit more to it. So, how is this accomplished? Figure 18.1 gives you a visual of what we are talking about.

At a basic level, an HR partner must be able to (1) execute processes and initiatives, (2) manage risks associated with people decisions and processes, (3) advise and coach business leaders, (4) provide HR-related subject-matter expertise, and (5) show the causal relationship between what Human Resources does and strategic business priorities. Although the previous profiles of what not to do focused on HR generalists, this model applies to both specialists and generalists. The only difference is the breadth of subject-matter expertise required. For example, a leadership-

Figure 18.1 HR Profiles with Business Priorities

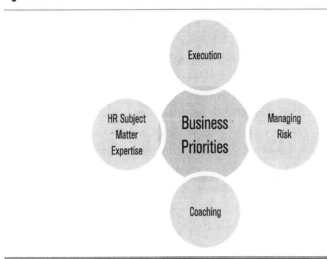

development consultant should have subject-matter expertise in assessing, selecting, and developing leaders.

We are sure that these five capabilities do not seem new or profound for any seasoned HR professional. The authors of *HR Competencies* showed us a compelling list of key competencies for HR professionalism.[2] This list included (1) talent manager/organization designer, (2) culture and change steward, (3) strategy architect, (4) operational executor, (5) business ally, and (6) credible activist. This coincides nicely with the profiles that we have discussed, so there is a good bit of consensus. Ulrich and his associates do a great job of outlining all of these in detail. The key addition is incorporating our approach of linking everything that an HR trusted advisor should be doing to key business outcomes — and doing it in a way that shows causality (passes research/statistical muster). However, the true wisdom of this Trusted HR Advisor model lies in two fundamental assumptions of the model:

1. The HR Trusted Advisor balances all of these competencies when performing his or her role.
2. It is acceptable to lead with one competency when it is a core strength, but neglecting any single competency will derail your path to "trusted advisor" status.

To be fully maximized, all five competencies are guided by and directly linked to business priorities and strategies. This sounds simple, and we all understand the importance of this notion, but rarely do HR partners consistently accomplish this task.

Given the content of this book, we are especially interested in the second point. The sole mission of this book is to help HR professionals take the linkage of people-focused activities and meaningful business outcomes to the next level. We want to move beyond a fundamental understanding that people are important, to establishing an empirical relationship between people activities and business results. When such data are empirically linked together, then and only then can truly fact-based decisions be made regarding people strategies and investments. As such, the achievement of Trusted HR Advisor status requires HR partners to not only qualitatively connect traditional HR activities to business activities, but to empirically link HR activities to business outcomes. We are not suggesting that every decision be made based on a quantitative study. Rather, we are suggesting that people strategies be built using quantitative data. Just like business strategies, this is typically done annually during the planning process.

Competencies

We are sure that you have seen numerous competency models for HR leaders, and you may have even developed them throughout your careers. Competency models can be great pieces of information to drive selection, training, development, performance appraisals, etc. Rather than build out another full-blown HR competency model, we just want to show you how incorporating the key aspects of the Business Partner RoadMap™ into your HR competencies can help to make you a better Trusted HR Advisor in your organization. Figure 18.2 walks you through some key areas to give you some insights regarding these competencies.

Figure 18.2. HR Competency Model

Competency #1

■ Demonstrate the causal relationship between what HR does and strategic business priorities

>> Conduct meaningful stakeholder interviews with senior leaders.

>> Facilitate meetings with key stakeholders from multiple areas of the business.

>> Align and consolidate various functional data from diverse areas of the business.

>> Analyze large databases using statistical techniques that demonstrate causality.

>> Analyze performance of the processes and initiatives to determine effectiveness.

>> Adjust and enhance processes and initiatives based on their impact on business priorities.

Competency #2

■ Pragmatically execute processes and initiatives

>> Build strategic programs that are evidence-based and have measurable outcomes.

>> Communicate complicated statistical analyses and results in common, actionable language.

>> Influence, without direct management authority, to gain line-of-business leaders' support for processes and initiatives.

>> Re-evaluate, and adjust processes and initiatives, based on periodic data analysis.

Competency #3

■ Manage risks associated with people decisions and processes

>> Demonstrate a practical understanding and application of relevant employment law.

>> Educate front-line leaders to understand the implications of HR decisions.

>> Guide leaders to make decisions that aid the business while minimizing risks.

>> Provide solutions to leaders that mitigate risks yet still accomplish desired results.

Competency #4

■ Advise and coach business leaders

>> Use facts, data, and analysis to guide leaders to decisions that positively impact the business.

>> Effectively communicate the relationship between people and business outcomes.

>> Demonstrate executive presence to gain credibility.

>> Demonstrate an understanding of how the business makes money in order to drive effective people-related decisions.

Competency #5

■ Provide HR-related subject-matter expertise

>> Demonstrate an understanding and practical working knowledge of HR subject matter.

>> Communicate HR expertise in actionable language.

>> Leverage HR expertise when developing people-related interventions that are linked to business outcomes.

CHAPTER 19

Concluding Remarks

For some, the whole "advanced statistical knowledge" requirement might appear to be a limitation/barrier to our approach. This is understandable, and this is also to be expected. Remember, the most important message for HR leaders is to use our process and approach to link employee data to business outcomes. This allows for the prioritization of opportunities and interventions, as well as a clear calculation of ROI. Therefore, the process described in the Business Partner RoadMap™ is the focus, not the statistics required to complete one particular step. That step can be performed by a partner or vendor. Like most "new" processes, the first application is the most difficult. Subsequent applications of the process are typically more efficient and effective.

Remember, when applying our process, Human Resources needs to always think like a front-line manager and the CFO at the same time. More precisely, we need to show the specific causes of what is important and then their financial impact on the organization. The process is straightforward to accomplish these goals. Effectively implementing this process in your organization should not only provide additional credibility to the HR function, but may also create a new level of accountability within the organization.

If you don't work in Human Resources, then request that HR leaders approach their jobs with this process, support them in their quest for data, and invest in what they will *prove* to you. Then come back to them — using data and analysis, of course — with the next problem/issue/investment that comes across your desk, because they will likely have some key input. The returns will materialize, the process will permeate throughout the organization, and Human Resources will become an internal consulting firm that many functions will seek out to help them reach their critical business outcomes. The "people report" might even lead-off your future board meetings and find a place on the balance sheet of your annual report.

"Our people are our most important asset" is nice to say, but it is even better to prove it and use it to improve business outcomes.

Appendices

Ten Guiding Principles

1. Organizations already spend significant amounts of money on their people ... they just don't spend it on the right things.
2. Organizations make investments in people without any data or with the wrong data.
3. Employee engagement in itself is *not* a business outcome.
4. People and organizations are complex. The linkages between attitudes and outcomes have to be understood within *your* organization using *your* data.
5. The people data and outcome data do exist — you just have to go and get it.
6. The organization's data exist in silos.
7. There will be obstacles and barriers to obtaining the data (e.g., politics, turf battles).
8. Once a connection/linkage is made with the data, accountability is unavoidable (and that's a good thing).
9. Don't assume a link between employee data and business outcomes — define it and understand why or why not.
10. Perceptions alone do not show up on the P&L statement.

Software

To get the job done and truly show the value and bottom-line impact of your people data, you will need to make some minor investments in statistical software. We recommend purchasing the SPSS/AMOS program (www.spss.com). This software gives you the ability to do some basic statistical analysis (means/averages & standard deviations) and somewhat more sophisticated analyses such as correlations and multiple regressions. These are all important analyses that can give you very important insights into your data. The AMOS program allows you to conduct the structural equations modeling (SEM) that is required to link multiple data sets together. Linking the multiple data sets is the key to showing the real impact in your organization. The AMOS program is what is needed to show the causal relationships between your organization's people data and the critical outcomes that drive the business.

To be clear, we are not compensated in any way by SPSS in recommending their product to you. We personally have used this product over many years, and it has proven to be reliable and capable of handling critical data and complicated analyses.

Personnel

We talked about a certain amount of "advanced statistical knowledge" being involved to conduct these analyses. However, before you think that you have to create an entire function full of Ph.D.s, take heart, the cost here will not be extreme. Sure, you will need to set up those CFDTs and have meetings and create presentations. But the actual analysis could be conducted by a professional statistician. However, for your organization, we do recommend a full-time Ph.D. in Industrial/Organizational (I/O) Psychology. Yes, a professional statistician will know how to do the structural equations modeling, but an I/O psychologist will have the requisite experience in not only statistics, but also in people metrics/behaviors and business. This is an important point, because once you discover how the things that you do impact business outcome, you will also want to have an individual who understands how to work on those important "things."

The Society for Industrial/Organizational Psychology (SIOP) is a division of the American Psychological Association (APA) (Division 14) and is affiliated with the American Psychological Society (APS). We are not giving SIOP a free plug here. Instead, we are providing you with a resource to learn more about the skills and competencies of I/O psychologists. We know that you are going to call the authors of this book if you need to get started with the approach in this book but, just in case, the SIOP web site (www.siop.org) has a "consultant locator" function to help you find a consultant and a "jobs" page if you would like to pursue full-time help. The SHRM web site (www.shrm.org) also has this type of functionality.

Areas of Competence to be Developed in Doctoral-Level I-O Psychology Programs.

1. Consulting and Business Skills
2. Ethical, Legal, and Professional Contexts of I-O Psychology
3. Fields of Psychology
4. History and Systems of Psychology
5. Research Methods
6. Statistical Methods/Data Analysis

7. Attitude Theory, Measurement, and Change

8. Career Development

9. Consumer Behavior

10. Criterion Theory and Development

11. Health and Stress in Organizations

12. Human Performance/Human Factors

13. Individual Assessment

14. Individual Differences

15. Job Evaluation and Compensation

16. Job/Task Analysis and Classification

17. Judgment and Decision-Making

18. Leadership and Management

19. Organization Development

20. Organization Theory

21. Performance Appraisal and Feedback

22. Personnel Recruitment, Selection, and Placement

23. Small Group Theory and Team Processes

24. Training: Theory, Program Design, and Evaluation

25. Work Motivation

Stakeholder Interview Guide

Before your initial cross-functional data meeting, it is critical to conduct stake-holder interviews. These interviews should involve you and all of the senior leaders (or senior leaders in your specific line of business). The goal of these interviews is to identify the truly critical outcomes that the organization is aiming for. Second, within this context, the interviews will help these key stakeholders understand that potential invisible levers could exist that can be pulled to enhance business outcomes. These interviews will provide both insights and buy-in for this critical journey on which you are about to embark.

Rather than leave you on your own to build these interviews from scratch, we have provided (below) an effective template of key questions that should be asked during the stakeholder interviews that will get you the information you will need to effectively launch and sustain your cross-functional data meetings.

Key Interview Questions

The following is a typical approach to introducing your goals for the interview with key stakeholders. You will, of course, need to customize this for your organization as necessary:

"As your HR partner, we would like to more closely align our initiatives to your critical business outcomes. In order to do that we need to understand (1) your business priorities, (2) what your related goals are, and (3) how they are measured. We then need to discover how HR initiatives and people data impact those business priorities. Our team will use advanced analytics to empirically connect the people data to the business data. In order to accomplish this, we will ask you and other senior leaders a series of structured questions. We ask for your support and input in gathering this information and in subsequent actions taken to impact your business priorities."

Business Priorities

- What are the strategic priorities of the organization?
- In your opinion, what are the most pressing issues facing this organization today? Are there issues facing particular segments of the business?
- What are your biggest barriers to overcome in addressing these issues/priorities?

Business Priorities – Goals and Measurement

- What measures/metrics are in place to show that progress is being made in these areas? What standards or goals have been set? How achievable are these goals?

People Priorities

- In your opinion, what are the most pressing issues facing the employee and customer population?
- How do these employee/customer issues impact business outcomes?

Business, Customer, and Employee Data

- Are there key data sets that you think should be analyzed to discover causal drivers?
- Do you anticipate any barriers to obtaining the data needed from the various functions to conduct these analyses?
- Is there anything else you can tell me to insure that the project is successful?

Structure/Agenda of the Cross-Functional Data Team Meeting

When conducting the cross-functional data team meeting, it is important to quickly demonstrate not only the goal of meeting, but also the value to the business that can be achieved by the participants. You will need to build a PowerPoint deck that articulates the following areas:

- Goal(s) of the Meeting
  - » Empirically link HR data to business-outcome data.
  - » Prioritize HR strategy based on business impact.
  - » Identify interventions and initiatives to drive the HR strategy.
- Advantages/Positive Outcomes of Participation
  - » Gaining additional levers to pull to impact functional outcomes.
  - » Employing HR's assistance to help reach your function's goals.
  - » Integrating data across functions to better align activities.
- Discussion of Linkage-Analysis Methodology
  - » Allows for examining multiple data sets and outcomes simultaneously.
  - » Higher level of sophistication beyond correlation and regression.
  - » Ability to infer causality and strength of impact.
- Strategic Initiative Review
  - » Summary of stakeholder interviews.
  - » Agreement on prioritization of stakeholder recommendations.
- Balanced Scorecard Review
  - » Review how current priorities are measured today.
- Critical Functional Metrics/Data Needs
  - » Based on priorities, discuss how data is measured for each area.
  - » Identify data owners and sources for each function.
- Next Steps
  - » Prioritize projects.
  - » Set timelines and accountabilities.
  - » Schedule follow-up meetings.

The Concept of Causality

Throughout this book, we have discussed how to determine the "key causal drivers" of business outcomes. This is certainly a departure from various texts that show correlations between what the HR department does and certain bottom-line indicators. Our goal at this point is not to get into an overly detailed discussion of statistical analysis; however, it is a great opportunity to discuss how we arrive at the phrase "key causal driver," and why it is important for you, the audience, to grasp this.

First, let us cover some of the academic aspects of this analysis.

1. *Theory.* In regard to academic research, a critical step to determining if a data is truly causal is that it must be based on solid theory. In an academic setting, this would typically mean citing a previously conducted study that shows some sort of statistical connection between similar data to what you would be looking at. This is absolutely a strong standard, whether it is from an academic or from a practitioner's perspective. If two variables (i.e., pieces of data) are linked together, it really needs to make intuitive sense or have some foundation in logical thought. We always propose that the models and analyses that you run are done in what is called confirmatory mode. This means that you set up how the data should look before analyzing, with the goal of confirming what you think should happen (i.e., your theory). The other mode of analysis is exploratory, which is where you throw the data into your statistical software and see where the data falls. Yes, you may make some interesting discoveries; however, if what is discovered is not based on logical reasoning or "theory," then you should never use the term "causal." For example, you may find that retail stores with higher turnover also have higher 401(k) plan participation. That's nice to know, but it makes little practical sense to start firing people so that you will have more people in the 401(k) plan.

2. *Correlation.* In a similar fashion, what we have proposed throughout this book is not a correlational analysis. Correlations are great to find a connection between two pieces of data. Correlations will only tell you whether or not if one variable's strength is associated with another variable's strength (or weakness to weakness). This analysis can show you the strength of the relationship, and if the relationship is statistically significant. Correlations do not demonstrate any type of causality whatsoever. The classic example of this is the connection between shark attacks and ice cream sales. There is truly no logical reason for these two aspects of life to be connected, but they just happen to be connected. Both occur with more frequency in the summer months. This is called a spurious correlation. Fair enough, but from a practical perspective, we do not believe that Baskin Robbins should start chumming the waters at the local beaches as part of their growth strategy.

3. *Including all Relevant Causal Variables.* Another key issue in determining whether a variable is causing another variable to happen is that you have included in that analysis all relevant causal variables. This means that you do not just include the variable that you hope is causing the business outcome but, rather, you have included all of the data that could possibly (based on logic, as discussed above) be a cause of the business outcome. In the grand scheme of things, it is humanly impossible to include every possible cause of a

business outcome. However, both academically and practically, if you include all of the data measured (and start measuring some key aspects that you have not measured in the past), you can make a strong inference and conclusion that a variable is a key causal driver of an outcome. This will pass muster in the boardroom and at even the most discerning peer-reviewed academic journal. The point is that you must make a strong, good-faith effort to measure all that you can, and include all of those measurements when you conduct the analyses.

4. *Accounting for Measurement Error.* When you are discussing with your team as to why you should use structural-equations modeling vs. less complex analytical techniques such as correlation or even multiple regressions, a key argument to make is that you will be able to account for measurement error. This is an important piece of information to have when you think about this analysis. With correlation and regression, which are strong analytical techniques, a key point is that you assume when you use these approaches that all data has been collected without any error. All data that is collected, particularly attitude data, performance ratings or ratings of behavior, have error associated with their measurement. Whether it was the bad weather the morning of the survey, the cold coffee, the systematic error associated with the validity of the survey items, or the rating scales in the online performance-appraisal tool, there is some error in that measurement. Structural-equations modeling gives you a more pure approach to the analysis because, in the analytics, you get to account for that error. This means that there is one less assumption that you have to make about the data that you are analyzing. Does this mean that you can automatically claim causality? No. But it does get you one step further, and if you incorporate the previous three steps, you can begin to make such inferences of causality.

As we have mentioned throughout the book, we did not want to write a statistics textbook and, thankfully, we have not. These Appendices are designed to give you some of the ammunition that you will need in the boardroom when you are asked questions about the process. Or, when a senior executive realizes that you just asked for a large sum of money for an important project that is based on these types of analyses. Those senior leaders are just doing their due diligence (which they should), but you need to be able to show them that you have also done your due diligence.

Endnotes

Chapter 1

1. Rucci, A.J., et al. (1998). "The employee-customer-profit chain at Sears," *Harvard Business Review*, Vol. 76 (1), pp. 82-97.

Chapter 2

1. GE Annual Report 2006.
2. GE Annual Report 2007.
3. Conoco Phillips Annual Report 2006.
4. Conoco Phillips Annual Report 2007.
5. Procter and Gamble Annual Report 2006.
6. Michaels, E., et al. (2001). *The War for Talent*. Harvard Business School Press, Boston.
7. Collins, J. (2001). *Good to Great: Why Some Companies Make the Leap... And Others Don't*. Harper Collins, New York.
8. AT&T Annual Report 2008.
9. "Accounting for Good People," *The Economist*, 19 July 2007.
10. Hansen, F. "New performance yardstick; When intellectual capital and institutional skills play a larger role in wealth creation than tangible assets, workforce-based metrics move into a new role," *Workforce Management*, May 7, 2007.
11. Aijala, A., et al. "Aligned at the Top." Deloitte and Touche, Sept. 2007.
12. Meisinger, S. "New Study Challenges HR, Illustrates Opportunity," *HR Magazine*, Nov. 2007, p. 8.
13. Buckingham, M. and C. Coffman. (1999). *First, Break All the Rules*. Simon & Schuster, New York.

Chapter 3

1. Schmitt, N., et al. (2003) "Personnel Selection and Employee Performance." In W.C. Borman, et al. (eds.) *Handbook of Industrial and Organizational Psychology*, (pp. 77-106): John Wiley & Sons, Hoboken, NJ.

Chapter 4

1. Organ, D. W. (1988). *Organizational Citizenship Behavior: The Good Soldier Syndrome*: Lexington Books, Lexington, MA.

Chapter 5

1. Covey, S. (1989). *The Seven Habits of Highly Effective People: Powerful Lessons in Personal Change*. Free Press. New York.

Chapter 6

1. Kaplan, R.S. and Norton, D.P. (1996). *The Balanced Scorecard: Translating Strategy into Action*. Harvard Business School Press, Boston, MA.
2. Rucci, A.J., et al. (1998).

Chapter 8

1. McFadden, M. & Demetriou, E. (1993). "The role of immediate work environment factors in the turnover process: A systemic intervention," *Applied Psychology: An International Review*, Vol. 42(2), pp. 97-115.
2. Zimmerman, R. (2008). "Understanding the impact of personality traits on individuals' turnover decisions: A meta-analytic path model," *Personnel Psychology*, Vol. 61(2), pp. 309-48.
3. Carsten, J. M., and Spector, P. E. (1987). "Unemployment, job satisfaction, and employee turnover: a meta-analytic test of the Muchinsky model," *Journal of Applied Psychology*, Vol. 72, pp. 374-81. Koys, D. J. (2001). "The effects of employee satisfaction, organizational citizenship behavior, and turnover on organizational effectiveness: a unit-level, longitudinal study," *Personnel Psychology*, Vol. 54, pp. 101-14. Gentry, W.A., Kuhnert, et al. (2008). "The influence of supervisory-support climate and unemployment rate on part-time employee retention: A multilevel analysis," *Unpublished manuscript.*
4. Vandenberghe, C. and Tremblay, B. (2008). "The role of pay satisfaction and organizational commitment in turnover intentions: A two-sample study," *Journal of Business and Psychology*, Vol. 22(3), pp. 275-86.
5. Fleishman, C. (1998). "Patterns of leadership behavior related to employee grievances and turnover: Some post-hoc reflections," *Personnel Psychology*, Vol. 51(4), pp. 825-34.
6. Williams, C.R. (1999). "Reward contingency, unemployment and functional turnover," *Human Resource Management Review*, Vol. 9(4), pp. 549-76.

7.   Cohen, A., and Hudecek, N. (1993). "Organizational commitment-turnover relationship across occupational groups," *Group & Organization Management,* Vol. 18, pp. 188-213. Currivan, D.B. (1999). "The causal order of job satisfaction and organizational commitment in models of employee turnover," *Human Resource Management Review*, Vol. 9(4), pp. 495-524. Gaertner, S. (1999). "Structural determinants of job satisfaction and organizational commitment in turnover models," *Human Resource Management Review*, Vol. 9(4), pp. 479-93.

8.   Bandura, A. (1986). *Social Foundations of Thought and Action: A Social Cognitive Theory.* Prentice-Hall, Englewood Cliffs, NJ.

9.   Eisenberger, R., et al. (1986). "Perceived organizational support," *Journal of Applied Psychology,* Vol. 71, pp. 500-7.

10. Mitchell, T.R., et al. (2001). "Why people stay: Using job embeddedness to predict voluntary turnover," *Academy of Management Journal,* vol. 44(6), pp. 1102-21. Lee, T. W., et al. (1999). "The unfolding model of voluntary turnover: A replication and extension," *Academy of Management Journal, 42,* 450-62. Lee, T. W., & Mitchell, T. R. (1994). "An alternative approach: The unfolding model of voluntary employee turnover," *Academy of Management Review, 19*(1), 51-89. Holtom, B. C., & Inderrieden, E. J. (2006). "Integrating the unfolding model and job embeddedness model to better understand voluntary turnover," *Journal of Managerial Issues, 18*(4), 435-52. Mitchell, T. R., et al. (2001).

11. Cook, K. S., and Rice. E. (2003). "Social exchange theory," In Delameter, J. (Ed.), *Handbook of Social Psychology,* Kluwer Academic/Plenum Publishers, New York, pp. 53-76.

12. Eisenberger et al. (1986).

13. Mitchell et al. (2001).

Chapter 11

1.   Ashkenas, R., et al. (1995). *The Boundaryless Organization: Breaking the Chains of Organizational Structure.* Jossey-Bass, San Francisco. Lencioni, P. (2006). *Silos, Politics and Turf Wars: A Leadership Fable about Destroying The Barriers That Turn Colleagues Into Competitors.* Jossey-Bass, San Francisco. Ostroff, F. (1999). *The Horizontal Organization: What The Organization of the Future Actually Looks Like and How It Delivers Value To Customers.* Oxford University Press, New York.

Chapter 14

1. Mondore, S.P., et al. (2009). "An in-action group level model of high involvement work: Testing the effect of high involvement work climate on indices of group effectives." Under review.
2. Interview with Phillip Rosenzweig. "The Myth of Employee Satisfaction," *Workforce Management,* 7 May 2007.

Chapter 15

1. Friedman, T. (2005). *The World is Flat: A Brief History of the Twenty-First Century.* Picador, New York. House, R.J., et al. (2004). *Culture, Leadership and Organizations: The GLOBE Study of 62 Societies.* Sage Publications, Thousand Oaks, CA.
2. "Once thrashed, now treasured," *Atlanta Journal-Constitution,* February 10, 2008.
3. Hammers, M. (2003). "Wanted: part-timers with class," *Workforce,* Vol. 82, pp. 18. Polivka, A.E., et al. (2000). *Definition, Composition, and Economic Consequences of the Non-Standard Workforce.* "The Prevalence of Part-timers," The SHRM Weekly Poll. 2005.

Chapter 17

1. Hammonds, K. "Why We Hate HR," *Fast Company,* August 2005, Issue 97, p. 40.
2. "Out Front: A Fatal Turn in the Workplace," *Workforce Management Magazine,* 10 Sept. 2007.
3. Accenture High Performance Workforce Study 2006.
4. SHRM 2008 Workplace Forecast Study.

Chapter 18

1. Maister, D.H., et al. (2000). *The Trusted Advisor.* Free Press, New York.
2. Ulrich, D., et al. (2008). *HR Competencies: Mastery at the Intersection of People and Business.* Society for Human Resource Management, Alexandria, VA.

Index

About the Authors

Dr. Scott P. Mondore is a managing partner of Strategic Management Decisions (SMD) and has significant experience in the areas of corporate strategy, talent management, measurement, customer experience, and organizational development. He has worked for years in internal management and consulting positions across a variety of industries, including transportation, health care, manufacturing, utilities, and hospitality.

Before co-founding SMD, Dr. Mondore served as the East Region President for Morehead Associates, a survey and human capital analytics company. Before joining Morehead, he worked as a Corporate Strategy Director and Talent Management Director at Maersk, Inc. He also worked as an Employee Relations Manager at UPS, focusing on employee assessment and measurement, as well as working as a consultant to large and small organizations in both the private and public sector.

He has also published scholarly articles on various topics, including employee turnover, employee safety, coaching, litigation, and leadership. Scott is an adjunct professor of psychology at the University of Georgia, and has held the same status at Fairleigh Dickinson University.

He holds a master's degree and doctorate in applied psychology from the University of Georgia and can be reached at smondore@smdhr.com.

Dr. Shane S. Douthitt is a managing partner of Strategic Management Decisions (SMD) and has more than 15 years of experience in the areas of measurement, talent management, executive assessment and coaching, and organizational development. He has practical experience across a variety of industries, including banking, manufacturing, utilities, pharmaceuticals, and information technology.

Before co-founding SMD, he was the Senior Vice President of Sales & Products at Morehead Associates, a survey and human capital analytics company. Before joining Morehead, Shane worked as a Human Resources Executive and Leadership Development Executive at Bank of America. Shane also worked as a consultant for Towers Perrin, specializing in the design and delivery of integrated HR systems. Prior to these experiences, Shane worked as a consultant at IBM, as well as holding various HR generalist roles.

He has published several articles on a variety of topics, including measurement, teams, individual differences and diversity, employee selection, group dynamics, and cultural openness.

He holds a master's degree and doctorate in applied psychology from the University of Georgia, as well as a master's degree in industrial/organizational psychology from the University of Tulsa and can be reached at sdouthitt@smdhr.com.